CONSTRUCTION
HICCUPS

Additional publications by DAN BARRUS

Everything I Needed for Life, I Learned as a Scout
Wyoming's Best Kept Secret
Hunting and Fishing Bloopers
Memoirs of a Rescuer on the Second Rescue of the
Willie and Martin Handcart Companies
Our Baker's Dozen (the story of the Tunney Barrus family)
—E-Book Only—
America's Favorite Past Time
Historical Novels:
Jeremiah 2020
Big Sky Vigilante
Gem State Warden
Paint Creek Prodigal
Cloud Peak Refugees (due out in 2019)

CONSTRUCTION HICCUPS

PART 1

DAN BARRUS

Construction Hiccups

Copyright © 2019 by Dan Barrus. All rights reserved.

No part of this publication may be reproduced, stored in a retrieval system or transmitted in any way by any means, electronic, mechanical, photocopy, recording or otherwise without the prior permission of the author except as provided by USA copyright law.

The opinions expressed by the author are not necessarily those of URLink Print and Media.

1603 Capitol Ave., Suite 310 Cheyenne, Wyoming USA 82001
1-888-980-6523 | admin@urlinkpublishing.com

URLink Print and Media is committed to excellence in the publishing industry.

Book design copyright © 2019 by URLink Print and Media. All rights reserved.

Published in the United States of America
ISBN 978-1-64367-843-6 (Paperback)
ISBN 978-1-64367-842-9 (Digital)

Non-Fiction / Self-Help Book
11.09.19

CONTENTS

Preface 7

Chapter One: So you want to be a Contractor 9
               A Composite Degree at BYU 11

Chapter Two: Construction Superintendent Step One 17

Chapter Three: Head Superintendent for Olive and
               Glenn Nielsen 32

Chapter Four: Manager for Taggart Concrete/Rocky
               Mountain Pre-Mix 44

Chapter Five: Skyline Construction 60
               Wyoming State Training School Chapel 63
               Boysen Boat Ramps 69
               Western Nuclear Acid Plant Expansion 71
               A True Finisher Comes Along 77
               Looking for a partner 83
               A Fifty-five foot Vibrating Screed 88
               Pioneer Square in Worland (Bell Tower) 91
               Steel Buildings (Wedgcor) 93
               Pioneer Square (Site Improvements) 95
               Commercial Remodeling 98
               Wyoming Pioneer Home Remodel 100

Ft. Washakie Medical Clinic	107
Shoshoni LDS Remodel	116
Lander Medical Clinic	118
Arapaho Clinic	131
Construction Manager for Shoshone Enterprises	140
Washakie Dam Re-construction	144
Estimator Full Time for the Shoshone Tribe	152
Scattered HUD Homes	157
Arapaho Tribal Complex in Ethete	161
Epilogue	165

PREFACE

While I was re-reading my first four books, the thought crossed my mind. Now that we know what he did in his free time, what did he do day in and day out to afford so many trips to the mountains? So I decided to share my experiences while building projects around the area as a contractor.

I was told by a friend, when I was in college, to pursue a field that you really enjoy doing in your spare time. I have always enjoyed building things from the backyard to forts across the street. I studied building construction while at school and been enthralled ever since.

As I began relating my construction stories, it became obvious that one book would not be enough. So I will be dividing the books in half. Construction Hiccups I will be set in the time frame as a contractor and Construction Hiccups II will be centered around the profession of Construction Management. The management of men and materials is a real science after all.

There is a very satisfying feeling in being able to stand back at the end of the day to admire what a good crew can build with the proper tools and a little bit of hard work. It is equally as rewarding to see what can be accomplished when managing people towards the same end result. It just takes a little longer to see the results sometimes.

I enjoy seeing new construction projects wherever I go. It is in my blood and I totally get excited when a new breakthrough in means and materials comes my way. I can only blame myself when I see every one of my children, both men and women, set up and organize their own shops. They can't wait until they are able to afford that shiny new piece of equipment that they have been keeping an eye on for months.

I am proud to see what they have picked up from their 'Old Man' over the years. If nothing else, but to be able to stand back and admire what they have created.

CHAPTER ONE

SO YOU WANT TO BE A CONTRACTOR

Ever since I have spent time in our sandbox, I have had more fun building roads and cities than playing with them. The fun of catching a vision of what the finished product would look like and then fashioning the materials available to produce the final product has captivated my imagination and talents. Building a tree house was always a lot more fun than playing in one. I would carry that same curiosity and drive with me through the next fifty years of my life.

The first taste I received of real construction was in building homes with Gwynn Construction. I was just a laborer hired to complete what our foreman assigned me. But at the end of each day, we could stand back and actually see what had been accomplished using our bare hands and a few power tools. There is a solid sense of accomplishment in following that profession in life.

A laborer's tasks are never done. And cleaning always seemed high on the list. I didn't think the job site would ever run out of dirt. It seemed like the more I swept up, the more dirt miraculously returned the next day. But all I really need to tell you, is that we were building in Wyoming. Wyoming is famous for its wind and Cody had more than its fair share to go around. Cody sits right at the mouth of the Shoshone River. Two valleys, the Northfork and the Southfork can really generate a windstorm when they put their minds to it. It seemed to be like a sibling rivalry with each one determined to out blow the other. But all that wind managed to redistribute the silt sand from the benches above Cody onto the floor of the house I needed to keep clean. That was my first assignment every day, while the carpenters shook out the extension cords and power tools.

I learned quickly how to carry a sheet of plywood over my shoulder. And we were always in competition to see which one of us could carry the most 2 by 4's at once. It isn't always the strongest but the most agile that would win. And slowly but surely I picked up the jargon of the construction crew. Phrases like knee wall and pony wall took on new meaning. Treated lumber or redwood plates with trimmers and headers all becoming a second language after just a few days. But trying to understand our foreman's dialect was the toughest test of all. Our foreman, Norman, was born in Sweden but he learned how to speak his broken English while living in Georgia. That presented quite the paradox; A Swede with a southern accent can really be a challenge to understand at times.

I worked with Mellie as a fellow laborer. He was a willing companion but only stood half as tall as I did. I am not real tall myself standing only five foot six inches tall. That would bring Mellie in at just under five foot tall. Well I guess that is a little more than half as tall, but he made up for his stature with his fire-red hair. Over the summer we became fast friends and we each had each other's back… always.

Mellie had a devious mind at times. But he never did anything to hurt or injure anyone. I can remember him finding an empty Skoal chewing tobacco can that had belonged to Norm. Instead of just tossing it into the closest garbage barrel, Mellie wanted to trick Norm with the find. By placing a little sawdust from our Celotex sheathing in the can with just the right amount of water, it looked and smelled just like the real thing. But when we presented the Skoal can to Norm, he glanced first at Mellie and then at me. Then he grinned a big tobacco stained grin and started to laugh. "How dumb do you two think I really am? Now get back to work!" We all had a good laugh at the innocent joke and promptly returned to our garbage detail.

Norm usually kept us pretty busy with important but incidental jobs. When it came time to insulate, he made sure we both got involved. Nobody likes to install fiber-glas insulation. But we didn't complain, we took on the task just like we were suppose to. But we were much too fast in completing the job assigned. Norm was busy with a framing correction and really didn't want us helping him at all. But we kept pestering him for a new job assignment. Finally, he turned and just blurted out,"Why don't you two just go dig a hole and then fill it up again?" We both looked at him for a couple of seconds and upon seeing that he was totally serious, we proceeded to locate our shovels and a soft place to dig.

As I remember the hole measured three-foot square and two and a half feet deep. Not to bad for thirty minutes of digging. Another fifteen minutes and we had the hole filled in again. We reported back to Norm who had finished his framing work. He could not believe his ears. We had actually dug a hole and filled it up again. He just turned away shaking his head and smiling from ear to ear. I am sure he will be a little more careful to gives a productive job from then on out.

The summer's work helped me learn the basics of wood framing. We framed three different homes that year. They ranged from a simple ranch style home to a split-level duplex and eventually a monster two-story custom home. I can still remember scratching my head over the use of trusses. I just couldn't understand how a bunch of 2 by 4's could be used to span 30 or 40 feet and take the place of 2 by 12 ceiling joists and 2 by 6 rafters properly spaced. I would learn how later on during my college years but for now I just participated in the hand erection of trussed roof construction.

A COMPOSITE DEGREE AT BYU

I became interested in two different areas upon enrolling at BYU. Building Construction and Architecture are closely related. I had spent many an hour working on Architectural plans and renderings during High School. I wanted to put those skills to work but on an upper level. My counselor at BYU was able to spark my interest in Industrial Arts. He sensed in me an ability to teach and help others in the classroom. But when he signed me up to attend a building trades class at the local high school, I was hooked. Together we charted my course using Industrial Education and Building Technology as composite majors. He set himself up as my mentor and supervisor for a degree that had never been pursued before at BYU.

The first thing he encouraged me to complete was a challenge course. By taking a test in a specific area of their core classes, I could add all those hours to my transcript at the grade I earned on the challenge test. I took the test and finished with a grade of 'B'. Most people would probably have been thrilled to receive 20 hours of credit at the 'B' level, but I chose to by-pass the extra credit knowing that I could do better.

I was carrying 18.5 hours while attempting to earn a starting position on the BYU baseball team. Almost everybody I talked to thought I was overloading myself and couldn't possibly maintain that schedule. But I had carried a full load while in High School, and played non-stop athletics at the same time. I had plenty of time for sports and studies since classes weren't held every day. I was living a short five minutes from the bulk of my classes and I had very little desire to socialize with the students my age. I was clipping along with a B+ average and had tons of spare time on my hands.

I decided to serve a full time mission following my first semester. I was called to the Colombia/Venezuela Mission. I served my entire mission in Colombia however. I thoroughly enjoyed Colombia and everything it had to offer. When I served, the drug cartels had not begun their reign of terror. The coffee plantations were the bread and butter industry throughout Colombia.

I returned to BYU after earning the necessary funds. I made contact with my Counselor and Mentor upon arriving back in Provo. We both picked up right where I had left off. The composite degree was still a possibility. But after just a short time, I noticed a disturbing trend to not finance the Industrial Education programs with the same gusto as before. In fact several of the High Schools that had been paramount in the Construction Trades limelight had totally dropped their programs all together. I had been watching the Heber High

School specifically. They had joined the ranks of multiple districts that determined the trades were a dying program on the secondary level!

As I neared completion of my college experience, Industrial Education had all but disappeared from many schools all together. I needed to make a decision and quick because my monies were been stretched to the limit. I had a family to care for. With two children with the last name of Barrus, I had to graduate. Full-time employment was a necessity and I was tired of the rigors that BYU presented. During my last semester, I decided to apply the knowledge I had acquired and get a construction job to help cover the costs.

A local contractor hired me to help frame houses. Kay and his sons must have grinned from ear to ear when they first saw me walk on to their building site. All decked out in new tools and a new belt full of the hand tools I had acquired. But after that first day however, I proved I could handle the work. I even had a few ideas and methods from my earlier framing job that they adopted to help make the projects easier and more cost effective.

As the summer was coming to a close, Kay was losing his help. His two sons still needed to finish High School and the work force in the area was dwindling fast. I was surprised when Kay approached me with his dilemma. He asked me if I knew any students that could fill the void. I spent a day looking around campus and came up short on any prospects. So I threw a twist at Kay. I felt that between the two of us, we could frame any house in the valley by ourselves. He thought about that for a few minutes and then blurted out," You know, I think we can too!"

Our next project would really put us to the test. Kay had contracted with a large contractor to frame several homes in the foothills above Pleasant Grove. The first one was a two story Southern style complete with massive columns for the front entry. Each day the home continued to take shape. A full basement was farmed which was followed by the main floor of the large home. As we started the framing for the second story, Kay threw a curve at me. The roof trusses were to be delivered in a couple of days. He had searched high and low for a crane to erect the trusses and the soonest anyone was available was still a week out!

We talked about taking a few days off while we waited for the equipment needed. But that would really put us behind schedule. As we talked we began to formulate a plan on how to erect the trusses by hand! We typically rolled the trusses into position with a lifting fork that Kay had designed. One man on the floor would roll the trusses, which were scattered out 'peaks down' to their final position with 'peaks up'. The other man on the crew would scamper along the roof nailing the trusses into place on the far side of the house and then spot nailing a layout spacer across the top of the roof.

All we had to do was get the roof trusses up to the second floor! We knew the flatbed truck that delivered the truss package had a tailgate height over four feet tall. By leaving a section of the wall open along the front for later, we planned on using the driver of the flatbed as an extra hand to slide those trusses up to us on the second floor. We would then slide each truss down the wall line in the proper order to be rolled into position later that afternoon. The driver was a little disgruntled that he had to physically help but after he understood the method, he really quite enjoyed the exercise.

I can still remember the construction supervisor showing up the following day. He was responsible for the equipment necessary to erect the trusses. He hadn't had any luck finding the needed equipment either. As he drove up to the house, which had all the trusses in place ready for the plywood sheathing, I was sure I saw his jaw drop an inch or two. He stood there for a couple of seconds and then he looked Kay straight in the eye and asked," All right, Kay, how did you guys get those trusses up there?" After a brief explanation, the superintendent volunteered to pass on the money saved to Kay and his 'Secret' crew. It was a real satisfying feeling to accomplish something many thought impossible.

The next couple of days were spent on lookout framing and sheathing the roof. It was while we were perched on the second story roofline, that we experienced a once in a lifetime accident.

The developer had contracted with a local dirt contractor to complete the street improvements. The curb and gutter had been in place for over a week and road gravel was being placed as fast as they could haul it in. That morning began just like the half dozen before. The road grader was fine-grading the small cul-de-sac where we were working. A steel drum roller was compacting the base course with an average sized water truck providing the much-needed moisture to the center of the main roadway.

About 10 A.M., the dirt crew decided to take a short break. They all bailed out of their equipment and congregated around the crew chief and his road grader. They must have been a hundred feet or so above us near the crest of the incline. As we were nailing off some of the higher eves on the roof, we caught a quick glimpse of the impending disaster. The water truck driver had failed to properly set the parking brake on the water truck he was driving. It was at least half full of water and was gaining speed as it rolled backwards past our observation point. The crew finally saw the truck just as it reached the end of the street. It had plenty of momentum and easily cleared the concrete curb and gutter that was blocking its exit.

The ridge that we were building homes on was at least a hundred feet higher than the gully floor directly below us. I saw the truck as it somersaulted its way down the side of the hill. It wasn't just rolling sideways down the incline but flying head over heel and gaining speed with each somersault. That truck was leaving divots a good twelve inches deep with each impact. Parts of the truck were being hurled left and right as the truck bounced its way to the bottom. When it finally reached the bottom of the ravine, it looked like a matchbox toy resting on its back. The dust began to settle as the crew stood and gaped at the sight. As the foreman checked to make sure nobody had been hurt, he exclaimed as loud as he could, "Holy Cow! Did you see that!" Needless to say there was plenty to talk about the rest of the day.

I was surprised that home construction still permeated my thoughts as I prepared to leave BYU. I received two legitimate offers following my graduation. I interviewed with a large commercial contractor based out of Salt Lake. They were widely known for their expertise in church owned facilities. In fact, they had recently completed work on two different temples outside of Utah. I was intrigued.

I also received a positive response from a small builder in Powell, Wyoming. He was interested in expanding his business into the commercial field. Jeanette and I definitely did not want to raise our family in Utah. So I accepted the offer in Wyoming. My footsteps were being guided but I did not realize it at the time.

CHAPTER TWO
CONSTRUCTION SUPERINTENDENT STEP ONE

I moved my family to Cody, Wyoming and promptly lost my first job in Powell. I made some mistakes and the Owner was not forgiving at all. That week was one I needed to forget as quickly as possible. We had previously loaded our two kids into our Ford Maverick and all our belongings into a medium sized U-Haul truck. Our plans were to make Cody by nightfall. But we were just leaving Meeteetse at dusk thirty miles behind schedule. I was pushing that truck as hard as I dare. But with an RPM governor, my top speed was 50 miles per hour and that was with a stiff tail wind. I did NOT see him approaching as we headed towards the Meeteetse Rim. A gigantic mule deer buck with massive antlers on both sides approached the highway I guess he thought he had the right-of-way because he crossed the highway just as I came upon him. He turned his head at the same instant that the truck plowed into him. Of course he lost the battle. But in so doing he did manage to thrush his antlers directly into the radiator of the U-Haul truck. We were both dead in the water. I jumped out to inspect the damage and put the buck out of his pain and misery. He was dead as a doornail! For whatever reason I decided to gut him and call the Game Warden. (That is a real task with only a small pocketknife) He noted the accident in his report and informed me that the meat would just go to waste. The state did not have any dead animal recovery program in place to salvage the venison.

We contacted my family in Cody and arrangements were made to get the family into Cody for the night. My brother, John, went with me to tow in the U-Haul truck the following day. I was certain they would charge an arm and a leg to tow the truck in by themselves. But when I finally arrived at the U-Haul dealer and sorted out the paper work. I did see a ray of hope. I had paid for insurance in Provo. All the towing and repair costs were covered! So we unloaded our belongings from the rented truck and moved on with life.

My next step was to locate suitable employment. It just so happened that Husky Oil Company was scheduled to break ground on their multi million -dollar corporate headquarters that summer. I made a few contacts and was employed by F.R. Orr Construction shortly there after.

Frank Burns arrived in town ready and able to get the project started. I learned from a seasoned superintendent how to get a field office set up and operational. He was a seasoned professional and I was as green as they come and straight out of college. But we hit it off right away. Not from anything that one would expect however. We became good friends while pitching horseshoes during our lunch breaks! We developed our own set of rules to keep things interesting. No, we did not play for money or anything close to that.

Our horseshoe games were set up so as to only count 'Ringers'. A ringer is worth three points and that was the only way to score was to throw a ringer. We did not count anything that wasn't a ringer. That meant no 'Leaners' or closest one to the pin scores one point. We would determine the advantage of pitching first by who had the most recent ringer. If there were no ringers on the South pit then the other man would be given the advantage on the North pit. It really sparked the competitive juices. We spent days pitching for Ringers or Nothing.

Orr Construction was a union contractor based in Denver, Colorado. They had won the contract over numerous In-state non-union contractors. They claimed that they could build the same building faster and cheaper than the non-union contractors because they had a pool of top Union sub-contractors and Union employees. And they set out to prove that point. Union vs Non-Union. I would benefit from that arrangement right from the 'Get Go'

I was a non-union laborer being paid identical wages as any Union Laborer in the state. And the wages were definitely better than the wages being paid by local contractors. But where more is given, more is expected. My training proved beneficial as to land me the position of Safety Instructor/ Head Laborer. The learning curve was set quite high and very rocky .I would learn quickly that the Union Halls did not favor having 'Scabs' working along side them on this or any other project. But when the Hiring Hall could not supply the needed help, the superintendent could reach out and hire the help he needed.

My first assignment from Frank was to work with the company surveyor to stake and layout the ten acres that would become Husky Headquarters. Gayle, the surveyor, arrived in town on a Sunday and was expected to begin work the very next day. There is a vast difference between suppliers in Cody as compared to Denver. This became very evident that first day. Construction lath and flagging that Gayle was used to buying next to their yard in Denver was not near the quality that the lumberyards sold in Wyoming. And Cody was far down on the list even among Wyoming suppliers. Gayle set about improvising. He handed me a machete and all the construction lath he had brought with him from Colorado. I spent the next two hours swinging that machete cutting a point on one end of two hundred laths. Gayle went shopping!

Gayle returned with a truck full of surveying paraphernalia. Four or five different colors of construction flagging, a case of permanent black markers, and a pickup full of sixteen-inch long wooden stakes were several that I would become personally attached to over the next few days. As I finished sharpening the last of the wooden lath, Gayle took a plot plan of the property and penciled in a fifty-foot grid over the entire sheet. He then produced a long skinny bag with a shoulder strap, which he told me to fill with the sharpened lath. He handed me a two-pound sledge and explained that we were going to drive a lath at every intersection point on the ten-acre site that corresponded to the grid he had penciled in on his plot plan.

We started out with a steel measuring tape that was locked in at fifty feet. Gayle then set up a transit on a point he declared his CONTROL POINT. From there he zeroed in on a distant landmark that corresponded to the surveying direction he had calculated. We then marched down that imaginary line while driving a lath every fifty feet. We followed this procedure for the next two hours until it time for our lunch break. We found some shade and proceeded to demolish the contents of our lunch boxes. As we sat discussing Cody and all that it had to offer, I made the comment about our work so far. It was something along the lines of "If we have to stake out the entire grid this way, it is going to take us the rest of the week!" Gayle cracked a smile and just said " Watch and learn, watch and learn!"

We then proceeded to eyeball the remaining spots using the measured points as a reference. Gayle would stand at a designated intersection an motion me right or left until I was reasonably close to the spot and then using an agreed upon sign I would drive a new lath at every intersection. I learned quickly how to Back Sight along the already installed lath to help speed up the process even more. By the end of the day we had the entire site staked and ready for the next days task.

That night Gayle pulled out his calculator and figured what the elevation needed to be at each intersection point on his fifty-foot grid. So when I arrived at the site the next morning, he was ready to begin shooting the existing elevations. He explained that once he learned what the existing elevation was for each of the grid points then he would transfer that into a CUT or a FILL designation. He also handed me several rolls of colored surveyors tape. RED will be used for the CUTS and BLUE will be used for the FILLS. He then handed me a walkie-talkie to attach to my belt. As I walked to each staked spot on the site, I would hold the graduated rod on the intersection point. Once Gayle had the reading, he would calculate the cut/fill and radio the result to me. I would in turn write the answer on the lath using either a "C" for cut or an "F" for fill. (Now I knew what the permanent markers were to be used for) The final instruction was to tie the appropriate colored ribbon on each lath allowing plenty of extra length to flutter in the wind. (That was to help the operators to see the lath more clearly.) By the end of the day we had a ten-acre site that resembled a cemetery on Memorial Day. A gigantic field of Blue and Red flags fluttering in the wind.

But when I arrived early the next morning, the flags and lath that I had hammered into the ground were NOT there! We had a wind during the night but nothing of any real consequence. The lath had NOT blown over! They were totally missing! We began a search of the entire site. Low and behold, we found every single solitary lath in a large pile on the Downhill side of the site. The entire two hundred laths had been gathered up, colored ribbons and all. They were all piled on top of each other. There were a few broken lath scattered around near this pile indicating that a make believe battle had taken place during the evening hours. The boys from the neighborhood must have had the time of their life using their lath as swords during their make believe battle. But the bottom line was that the past three days of survey work was totally ruined! The only way to move forward was to rework the entire ten-acre site again. But this time around Gayle had me drive a wooden stake along side each lath, as we re-staked the entire construction site. I hoped that this wasn't an omen of what else might happen during this construction project.

Harris Equipment had been hired to perform all of the excavation work. Once the staking was in place, they moved their scrapers and bulldozer on site. The topography of the site was transformed into the future Husky Oil Headquarters by the operators in determining the Cuts or the Fills needed to level the ten-acre site and to conform to the Engineer's design utilized the staking. I was assigned the task of maintaining the integrity of the grid that Gayle and I had staked out. Gayle repeatedly explained to each operator the importance of NOT hitting the lath and informing us when something seemed off kilter a little. But I only saw Gayle correct one station and that was only by a few tenths. Any time an operator noticed a colored ribbon missing, I was sent to that cross-section to replace the missing flag.

Following the rough grading of the site, the building corners themselves were staked out. Since the excavation for a twenty-foot deep basement was needed, a twenty-five foot offset was used for the batter boards. The outside corners received two batter boards,,, one offset to the North and the second one was offset to the East or the West depending on the orientation needed. All the inside corners were located using a single stake that was painted red. From this corner staking, an excavation line was identified using powdered baseball chalk. I think we bought every bag in town. This building was designed with the concept of a window for every office. And with forty or fifty offices, there were at least that many corners. Compound that with the fact that a second story was needed to house all the departments. It was the largest office complex in Northwest Wyoming by far.

The project was moving along slowly but surely. The next two months were consumed with digging and placing the footers. A Union carpentry crew was brought in along with a Union crew of ironworkers. Yes, I said ironworkers because all the rebar that was placed in the foundation had to be sorted out and tied in place by that specialized division. Union rules did not allow carpenters to handle any of the reinforcing steel. The laborers could assist both trades but the trades had a very definite division line between what could and could not be performed. The carpenters were commonly known as the ' Wood Ticks ' and the ironworkers were labeled 'Rod Busters ' Needless to say there was friction between these two trades.

The footers were nearing completion and a system of 'site built' wall forms was incorporated. Form Ply and Snap ties were imported by the truckload to accommodate the twenty-foot high walls that needed to be poured next. A panel system of sorts was developed to speed up the construction time line. Panels were built that measured eight feet wide by twenty foot long with a total of sixty panels needed for the first wall pour. The carpenters had a crew assembling the panels and another crew erecting each wall. The inside face of the panels were erected first. The reinforcing steel was then tied in place and secured to these forms. When the rebar was in place, the erection crew would 'button-up' the wall section by erecting the outside forms. Once that was completed a bulkhead was placed at both ends of the pour to be used for a continuation of the foundation work.

I will never forget what happened next. The first wall pour was set for nine o'clock the following morning. But during the night, one of those famous Wyoming gales arrived with winds in excess of fifty miles per hour. It blew hard all night long. By morning however the winds had blown themselves out. When we arrived at the job site, we couldn't believe our eyes. The wall forms and rebar had all been blown down during the night. All that remained was a nasty configuration of plywood, two by fours, and number five rebar laying every which away. It reminded me of a giant game of 'Pick-up Sticks'! So instead of pouring two hundred yards of concrete, we all began disassembling the mess. It would cost the project another week of precious time and the financial cost of the ruined forms and rebar.

We had lost very valuable time during the summer months for a multitude of reasons. The bottom line was that external heat would now be needed to protect the freshly poured concrete from freezing. So another step was needed in the foundation construction. Reinforced plastic was used to build tents around the forms while large propane fired heaters were imported along with propane storage tanks periodically spaced around the foundation. I was sure their builder's risk insurance helped pay for all the increased costs. All the laborers were pleased that their jobs during the winter months would continue.

During the winter months, I learned a lot of the in's and the out's of site-built formwork. I spent hours building temporary heating enclosures. The Wyoming winds did not cooperate in the slightest. But progress was being made. Towards the first of the year, the union Ironworkers went on strike for a better contract. I was to experience first hand what a union strike was all about. Picket lines were set up at our job site entrances complete with banners and hand held picket signs. Dozens of striking 'Rod Busters' manned the picket lines twenty-four hours a day and seven days a week! At first the strikers were allowing non-union workers to cross the picket lines to work their shifts. The union carpenters were honoring the strike and refused to cross the lines. But things took a turn for the worse. The ironworkers on the picket lines decided to take things into their own hands. They began refusing access to the jobsite to any 'SCABS' (non-union workers) that tried to enter the job. The superintendent, Frank, was a card carrying carpenter for years and he had seen enough. Wyoming is a 'Right-to-Work' state. Which gives everybody the right to work, whether union or not. The laws of the state protect that right. Frank proceeded to inform the striking ironworkers that they could only picket at one entrance while the other entrance would be for public access. The strikers refused to comply. So the local sheriff was invited on to the scene. It only took one striker handcuffed and escorted to the 'Gray Bar Hotel' to get the public entrance opened up again. The strikers were given their choice of which entrance they could picket. Of course they picked the most visible entrance. So the non-union workers and general public had to enter and make deliveries using the West gates. And those gates were locked during the non-working hours.

But the Strikers were not to be outdone. They took it upon themselves to enter the building site during the non-working hours to sabotage the progress of the foundation work. It started quite innocently with the pilfering of incidental tools and equipment. But increased to vandalism and destruction of property. Frank caught several ironworkers in the foundation area late one night punching holes in the foundation forms and scattering materials all over the place. He placed a call to the Sheriff and the guilty parties were locked up until a judge had time to rule in the case. A hefty fine was imposed and the guilty parties involved were not allowed to set foot on the property for ten years. The situation was growing more intense by the day. The picket lines resulted to verbal abuse of cars and people who chose to drive along the main road that led in front of the jobsite. Of course anybody that had witnessed this abuse, learned to re-route and follow a different road to perform his or her tasks. The local newspaper gave the strikers plenty of attention for a week or two, but that was even dwindling. Thank heaven the strike ended quickly. A new contract was signed with the union workers!

But every cloud has a silver lining. Following the incidents that occurred during the strike, the union carpenters from around the area could not supply the needed trained crews to keep the project on schedule. The union hiring hall out of Casper sent a representative to Cody to recruit carpenters / apprentices to satisfy the demand to finish the Husky Oil project on time. I was invited to apply. I informed them that I was not interested in their apprenticeship program. They set up a panel to judge whether I was qualified to join as a full member. I was grilled for two solid hours on knowledge of carpentry ranging from terminology, common practices, and abilities. I did have some time served on union projects but was considerably short of their minimum requirements. Following this panel review, I was vetted on references and past performance. The bottom line was gratifying. I was placed on the roles as a full member of the Wyoming Chapter of the Carpenter's Union! The increase in salary more than paid for the monthly dues and I was enrolled immediately in their full benefit package! This was to prove very timely because my wife, Jeanette, needed major surgery and I found out that it would be completely covered.

The surgery that Jeanette needed was performed in Billings, Montana by a surgeon who was only a small handful qualified to complete the task. During Jeanette's recovery, I inadvertently dropped a heavy toolbox on my foot breaking my big toe and needing stitches. There I was trying to help around the house and entertain my two older children while on crutches. Jeanette was recovering from surgery and nursing our third child. We needed help! Jeanette's mother saved the day or should I say month. She came over from Idaho and took over in the kitchen. She was a lifesaver. Slowly I healed and was able to return to work. Jeanette completely recovered from her surgery and the three children continued growing like weeds.

But a couple of things did happen during that stretch. We were living in a house that had two stories. The main floor was on the second story and had an open stairway leading between floors. Jeanette's Mom insisted in covering the open rails of the railings with something to prevent the children from falling through. (She had probably heard of my frequent falls as well) So I relented and covered the handrails with the cheapest thing I could think of. Chicken Wire…yes, we stapled a three foot wide roll of Chicken Wire across the area we thought posed the greatest danger. (If that wasn't a Redneck solution, I guess I haven't seen one)

About this same time I received a birthday present of a rifle and a scope to use with it. The Bushnell scope came packed with small packets of a moisture absorbent gel. We didn't think too much about them at the time but live and learn. Danny Lyn and Jesse my two oldest children found that container of gel caplets and did what any normal child would do. They began eating them! When we found them with the half full container of those gel caplets, we were horrified. We promptly called the Poison Hot Line and rushed the children to the Emergency Room for help. After seeing the sample of gel caplets and talking for what seemed like an hour, the nurse at the hospital came in with a dozen small bottles of chocolate milk. Chocolate Milk? Yes, chocolate milk. Apparently the only possible consequence of consuming those gel caplets was dehydration. So the solution was to keep fluids moving through their systems. But we as their parents were given a very strict lecture about leaving all unusual containers out of children's reach. Research has shown that children who had treated for poison consumption once, very often are repeat offenders. I only hope that the next time my kids want some chocolate milk, they just ask for some instead of eating more gel caplets.

The Husky Corporate building project continued to move forward. I still see in my mind's eye the 'RED' flannel one-piece underwear that flew from the highest steel column as a sign that the steel erection was complete. Framing, sheet rocking, and trim work began at a furious pace. There were three floors in the building and a crew chief was assigned to each floor. It was not unusual to see framing proceeding on one face while electrical, plumbing, and insulating were in close pursuit. The walls were enclosed as quick as humanly possible. I still marvel at the multitude of paint colors that were incorporated into the menagerie of offices, hallways, and waiting rooms. I was really glad I was not in charge of getting the right colors on the right walls. I was informed that Olive Nielsen herself was the interior designer. She was known far and wide as a designer that was difficult to please.

Two of the rooms that I specifically remember were at opposite ends of the building and also on different floors. The corporate computer room was located in the lower level. Keep in mind that this project was built in the late 1970's and the computer world was much different than we have in 2016. The computer room was the size of a small gymnasium. The main walls were erected so as to be totally sound proof. A six-inch thick wall with staggered studs and sound insulation was employed. But it was the floor that really caught my attention. The eight-inch concrete floor was in place and then a special seismic modular lattice grid was installed. The floor itself stood twenty four inches above the concrete floor allowing for computer cabling and power troughs to feed all the equipment that was to make up the 'Brains' of the Corporate Accounting System from underneath. There was more time spent on this one room than all of the other rooms combined.

Of course the President/ CEO's wing was a step above everything else in the building. Custom built-in cabinetry was installed everywhere. Solid oak crown molded ceilings were placed in this room as well as the board of directors room. The latest electronic devices of the day were implemented in this wing. The Husky Oil Corporate Logo was stitched into the carpets and rugs throughout. The furniture used here was imported from a custom shop in Los Angeles that was hand selected by Olive Nielsen.

As an Assistant Superintendent, my involvement was to direct and supervise the extensive site work of the remaining ten acres. It was designed along the lines of an exclusive golf course. Soft undulating hills covered with small groves of native aspens and pine trees were located sporadically around the site. An asphalt walk path meandered lazily over the grounds with lush green sod laid everywhere. But the most remarkable feature was the interconnecting lakes that enclosed three sides of the building. They were man-made and were to serve a very specific purpose above just being beautiful to look at. The water used to fill all three lakes and waterfalls was to be used as the cooling feature for the buildings. The water from the furnaces was released into the upper lake at one temperature and allowed to flow completely around the site over two water falls and eventually be re-used to cool the building at the lower end. That was quite ingenious if I do say so myself.

The lakes were to be lined with a product that Husky Oil Company sold throughout the Western United States. ASPHALT! The waterfalls were to be man-made using large boulders that had been unearthed during the site leveling process. Each boulder would be positioned strategically at the mouth of each lake and connected to each other by means of interconnecting concrete weirs. The workmanship was fascinating to supervise. But all great designs always seem to have hidden flaws and this was no exception. The flaw that was discovered late in the project was the asphalt itself.

Asphalt is not designed to be waterproof but just water-resistant. Asphalt is comprised of uniformly graded aggregate ranging in size from half-inch diameter all the way down to the finest of sands. This mixture is then coated with hot oils manufactured to bind all the aggregates together into a pliable mass. This mixture is then placed over a compacted base of sands and gravel to the designed thickness. If any of these steps are compromised then the product fails.

We did not encounter failure until the day following the filling of all three lakes with water. Thousands of gallons of irrigation water were used to fill the lakes. They were filled and allowed to flow as designed. It was truly magnificent to watch and observe. But upon arriving on the jobsite the following morning was a sad, sad experience. Each of the three lakes was totally devoid of any water. And a large failed section of the asphalt matt in each lagoon had failed some time during the night causing all the water to drain out!

The engineers were devastated but they all went back to work on a better design. The next lagoon design was to incorporate a twelve-inch layer of Bentonite (clay) directly below the asphalt matt. The Bentonite was available from quarries located near Lovell a mere fifty miles away. The whole process was repeated using this improved design. The result was another failure! Asphalt is not waterproof!

The final attempt to complete the lagoons was to utilize a waterproof membrane into the design. The expense was astronomical but the project was completed. But let me relate a short side story about the lagoon's design. The parking lot for all the employees and visitors was on the opposite side of the site from the building. The stream flowing between the first two lakes had to be crossed over. Yep, a bridge had to be built over the stream itself. Concrete was used exclusively and it was designed and constructed perfectly. On the building side of the bridge was a large concrete entrance cast using exposed-aggregate flatwork. It incorporated a five-foot grid of interconnecting concrete work. Scattered across this entrance were several features. Three flagpoles along with numerous benches were installed.

As I was observing the last pour of this two hundred foot square entrance, a unusual thing happened. Towards the end of the finishing procedure, we received an unwanted visitor. No it wasn't a neighborhood dog or cat, but a magpie that had been trained to talk. It flew into the fresh concrete and began hopping around leaving footprints wherever he went. When we yelled at him trying to get him to leave, he began imitating or yelling sounds by "yelling" back. And to top it all off, when we began laughing at his high pitch imitations, he just imitated or laughing with his own "laugh". It was all quite comical as I think back on the episode but very frustrating at the time. The bird was sent flying and the concrete work was repaired

Near the completion of this huge project, I was promoted to Head Superintendent over the Olive/Glenn Country Club project. But before this project could break ground, a massive clean up was needed at the Corporate Headquarters site. I supervised the collection and relocating of forms, lumber, and materials that I felt could be used on my new project. But even then, there was a gigantic mountain of debris that needed to be hauled away. That combined with the total cleaning of the new building presented quite the challenge. In Cody there were not any cleaning companies near large enough to accomplish the task. But one of the new grounds Supervisors from Husky Oil submitted a novel proposition. Why not hire the local LDS ward to clean the building and dispose of the unwanted materials and pay them the prevailing minimum wage! They claimed that 200 or more bodies could be on site by Saturday to begin if not complete the task. The idea was approved and the Saturday was set.

I was in charge of coordinating the manpower and logging the hours consumed. I was to find out very soon that I would have my hands full. People began arriving at the Husky building around 7 A.M. The first thing that was suggested was a short tour of the building itself before the cleaning was to begin. I wasn't part of the tour entourage and it was a good thing. There were close to three hundred people from the ages of twelve to sixty years old on site. Many of them I knew personally but there were dozens who I had never seen before. It resembled a herd of sheep that were waiting to be fed. They followed the tour guide all around in a tight bunch of arms and legs. They seemed a little afraid to touch anything in fear of damaging it.

That was to end very quickly however, as small cleaning groups were organized and given their assignments. I have never seen cleaning supplies disappear so efficiently. The General Contractor was responsible to provide all the appropriate solutions, rags, brooms, and mops needed. The two hundred plus cleaners poured back into the building with one goal in mind. Clean it from Top to Bottom! The remaining men and boys tackled the left over materials with gusto and every truck and trailer in their possession. Load after load of rebar, dimension lumber, plywood, steel beams, glu-lam beams, and fasteners were loaded and hauled to the homesteads of each and every worker.

About lunchtime, a large contingent of elderly ladies arrived with a caravan of station wagons filled to the brim with foodstuffs and gallon upon gallon of fresh lemonade. I didn't think it possible to feed three hundred people in less than thirty minutes. But seeing is believing! And just as quickly as the workers assembled for lunch, they returned to their assigned tasks with the same gusto as before. Frank, the Superintendent in charge, couldn't believe his eyes. By the time the sun was beginning to set in the West, the last load of scrap lumber was leaving the gate. The Husky Oil white glove inspection team concluded their work a mere thirty minutes later and awarded the grade of A+ to everybody's satisfaction! The Corporate Headquarters was ready for the move-in and the LDS Welfare Budget was bulging at the seams. Something of a modern day miracle!

CHAPTER THREE

HEAD SUPERINTENDENT FOR OLIVE AND GLENN NIELSEN

    Several years before I returned to Cody with my degree, Billy Casper designed and supervised the Cody Golf Course. It was quite an upgrade from the small 9-hole course located near the Upper Sage Creek. The new course was moved to the undeveloped lands just South of town. It was a professional grade 18-hole course un-matched in Northern Wyoming. But the tiny clubhouse that serviced that course was definitely sub-par. Enter Olive and Glenn Nielsen, the founders and primary owners of Husky Oil Company.

    They hired the same contractor that had just completed the new Husky Corporate Headquarters to design and build a Clubhouse that would serve the course and the community. I was promoted to Head Superintendent over this project. I can remember the very first time that I examined the construction drawings. A Clubhouse on the main floor of the building with a full basement set aside for cart repairs and parking. But that is where the golf facilities ended and the community benefits were displayed. On the main floor connected to the golfing locker room facilities was attached a twenty- meter swimming pool equipped with a Whirlpool-Jacuzzi. But it didn't stop there. On the West end was a full restaurant with two separate dining rooms and a kitchen to die for. Ample parking for golfers and dinner guests was out front and gorgeous landscaping to boot. I could hardly wait to get started.

The excavation and foundation work were completed in anticipation of the floor system delivery. The building was designed for a sixty-foot clear span pre-cast floor panels. They were cast in Billings, Montana and needed to be crane set from off the transport trucks. The date was set and we were ready! The placement went just as it was planned. The steel erection was next. Now where are those Beams and Columns anyway? It was a good thing they were delayed a couple of days. It gave us time to completely backfill the entire deep foundation. I made a decision on the steel erection that was very cost efficient. Instead of using a crane to erect all the steel columns and wood glu-lam beams, I chose to use a company-owned reach lift tractor that would be on site for the duration of the project. I checked with the pre-cast outfit in Billings to make sure their pre-cast panels could handle the concentrated floor loads. No problem! But you should have heard the whining from the project manager in Denver. Oooo-eeee! (The cost savings was in the thousands. Cody doesn't have an over abundance of cranes available)

But to begin the framing, a small obstacle needed to be overcome. The pre-cast panels are cast with a camber in each panel. In order to have a perfectly flat surface to set the wall framing on, we had to hand pour and place a leveling compound on the concrete panels exactly where all of the interior walls would be located. The pre-cast panel engineer wanted a leveling bed cast over the entire floor but my engineers in Denver decided against that. (We would pay for that as will be shown) But with the leveling bed in place, the walls went right up. They tied in nicely with the columns and beams that were already in place.

The sixty-foot truss package had been delivered a few days previous. Again the availability of a crane was looming in front of me. I had a good eight-man crew ready to proceed. And following a crew safety meeting, we decided to hand- erect the trusses. I had a custom truss turner fabricated similar to the one I had used in Utah. We carried all the trusses inside the building setting on the exterior walls with their peaks down. But upon attempting to turn that first truss into position, we noticed the gusset plates that were used in the fabrication were pulling apart. After a quick meeting of the minds, my union carpenters slapped a couple more truss turners together using wood instead of steel and we were in business again. Again hundreds of dollars were saved in eliminating the use of that crane. When Larry, our Project Manager arrived, he was dumbfounded that we had the framing complete and ahead of schedule and under budget as well.

I then split the crew with a framing crew working on the main building and a foundation crew to form and pour the swimming pool wing. I decided to pour the pool itself first and then follow behind that with the exterior walls. A few more sheets of form-ply would be needed but pouring the entire pool perimeter without a cold joint was to our advantage. The floor of the pool was poured monolithically. That was my first experience with the use of Water-stop. The joint between the floor of the pool and the walls had to be completely waterproof. The water stop itself and a welding wand were shipped up from Denver. We performed a few practice welds before the final weld was used. I was glad we had practiced on some small pieces first. It is a little different trying to man handle 3 feet of 12-inch water stop as opposed to two hundred continuous feet of the stuff.

The pool wall pour was next. I paid a little extra for a plasticizer in the concrete mix. It would allow us to pour with a higher slump and also slow down the hydration in order to achieve a pour without any 'honey-combing' or 'cold-joints' The 75-yard pour went very well. This was followed up with the exterior footings and wall. My concrete crew worked well together. While the pool concrete was gaining strength, my crew formed and poured the access ramps down into the basement. With the basement floor having been poured earlier in the project, the building was moving along quite nicely.

We had a deadline to meet. The owner had purchased clay-roofing tile in Chicago to be used for the roof. And it was due next month. We had the pool framing and trusses to set first. But I felt we had to get the structural fill placed around the perimeter of the pool before the wood walls could be erected. That decision was to prove costly.

The four semi loads of rustic clay tile arrived on schedule. We still had a week's worth of work on the rough framing to be ready for the installation to begin. This roofing tile was a kiln-dried product and had a flat profile as opposed to the Spanish style half-domed shape seen in many places. The roofer was from Montana and he arrived shortly after the product was delivered to Cody. The very first thing that he noticed was the color tinting was different between truckloads. The manufacturer was notified. He did indeed verify that the loads were from different runs at the plant. Every run has its own color tinting. There is no way to perfectly match the color tinting to any given run. And the next run wasn't scheduled for another two months! The manufacturer's recommendation was to mix the batch colors randomly as they are laid.

In order to do this the various pallets of tile would need to be spread out on the roof at the same time. Then the roofer could randomly select tiles that were from different runs and blend the mis-matched colors in to conceal the discrepancy. A small trial area was laid with the owner approving the 'blended' pattern. Things were back to flowing smoothly. The East face was laid and the West face had three or four pallets of loose tile scattered out across the surface. The scene was set for another Wyoming gale.

Yes, that afternoon the winds decided to cut loose. Winds measuring over 75 mph moved down the canyons and hit the jobsite. All we could do was to sit and watch the wind shred everything that wasn't nailed down. Whole sheet of three quarter inch plywood were flying across the yard. We sat there and watched as clay tile after clay tile was picked up from the windward side of the roof and in turn blown over the ridge to land on the already roofed leeward side. The flying tile would explode as they landed on the finished side and totally damage the laid tile wherever they happened to land. There wasn't a thing we could do to prevent the damage!

The next day, after the wind had died down, we ran a quick assessment of the damage that had occurred from the storm. The roofer and my crew all agreed that at least fifty percent of the tiles had been affected. If only we had that week back where we had taken time to place that structural fill. It would have cost a little extra but now we were looking at a major set back in both time and money. My project manager was aware of the storm and was timidly awaiting my assessment phone call. He stammered fifty percent at least three times on the phone. He then asked to talk to the roofer. They spent al least thirty minutes discussing options while I sat there completely mystified.

Larry told me to clean up the rest of the site and he would have the solution for me when we were finished. What a mess! It took the better part of the day to sort through the strewn materials and secure what we could. A couple of sixteen-foot trailer loads of trash were hauled to the landfill. We even got to know the neighbors better as we delivered toys, gardening equipment, and a couple of barbeque grills back to their rightful owners. That phone call from Denver didn't come until well past 6 P.M.

The only bright side to the whole affair was from Chicago. They still had enough tile left from their stockpile to replace the lost tiles. And they even had a repair procedure that had been used around Chicago. (Chicago is known as the Windy City) A dozen cases of a cooper repair brackets were being overnighted to us so repairs could be started immediately. I listened to Larry's explanation on the procedure to follow but got lost after the first two sentences from him. I knew that I would need to call the manufacturer and put them in touch with our roofer so there would be no confusion. The brackets showed up as promised with the replacement tile arriving a week later. The roof was salvaged! I was never told the final insurance amount claimed from that Cody Cyclone, but I was sure it was in the high thousands of dollars.

It was during this period that I would personally begin working closely with Olive Nielsen. She was well known around the community and the Western United States. She was at least twenty years older than I was. She was a very formal and proper lady. And she was very used to getting her way. Larry, our project manager, learned quickly that "NO" was not what she wanted to hear when discussing any of her ideas. She knew what she wanted and it was our responsibility to figure out how to achieve that end solution. I was to witness this principle in action time and time again. After all 'Money was no problem at all'.

This was very evident when the masonry work was to begin on the building exterior. Olive had approved a white 'slump' block to be used throughout. The mason was required to construct a 'mock-up' of the masonry wainscot that would be approved for the entire perimeter of the building. The mason that Larry had hired was from Worland, a short sixty miles from Cody. He had the sample wall panel ready for Olive's inspection. Larry, Olive, the mason, and myself were present for the approval of the very well laid block. The first words coming out of Olive's mouth were, "I don't like it!" The mason began to argue with her over trivial items. Olive then turned right in front of everybody there and asked Larry, "Where are the Swedes from Lovell?" Larry responded, " They were too expensive for the work to be done here." Olive then replied rather abruptly, " I will only accept work done by the Swedes! Get them hired right this minute!" The tension was as thick as molasses! The mason spun around and stomped off the job. Larry began stammering and apologizing to Olive. It took a few days but the next thing I knew the Swedes were on the site, laying block.

While the masonry work was progressing on the exterior, the interior utility work was in full swing. The electrician, plumber, and HVAC people were working hard to get it ready for the sheet rocking which was to start the following week. I was working with the plasterers in the pool area when Olive walks in. She asks me to take a short walk with her. As we walked towards the front of the building, we stop right in front of the completed fireplace. She looks straight into my eyes and tells me that she had just purchased a weather vane and a wood burning stove insert that she wants installed. She has decided on a 'Stagecoach ' theme and the weather vane and the insert have that in common. I was about to object but remembering the episode with the mason, I informed her that it might set us back a few days but that we would be "Happy to Include Her Ideas"

After she had left, I found my lead electrician and informed him that we needed to install a weather vane on top of the roof. He looked at me like I had totally flipped my lid. "Do you know what is involved in the installation of a weather vane to code?' was his immediate reply. " I know they have to have a lightning rod." Was my innocent answer. His tart response was, " And how do you propose to do that?"

I was to learn all about lightning rods in the next couple of days. The size of grounding cable needed, the special clamps needed, and the depth the rod has to buried in the ground were the easy details. The shortest route from the weather vane to the ground was the tough answer. With exposed beams and finished ceiling panels already in place, the task was daunting. I drafted my smallest laborer and with the use of the electrician's fish tape, we began to find a clear path to the ground (the bare grounding wire had to be totally concealed all the way to the grounding rod). After three hours of crawling, inching, and doubling back time after time; we finally had the route identified. It would only take four times as much grounding wire as is typically needed. The electrician was given the route we had identified and told to keep track of his total costs for this 'extra'.

The fireplace insert was actually the easier of the installation 'extras'. I nearly fell off my chair when I found out how much she had paid for this wood-burning stove. The only good part was Kenny, the dealer, would complete the installation at his own expense. I was pleased at the final appearance of this 'Stagecoach' themed stove with the brass coach on the front door and the weather vane was very appropriate as it sat looking down on the developing site.

One of the features of the Country Club was to be the whirlpool. It was to have tapered walls as it gradually sloped to the seating area that completely encircled the Jacuzzi. It was to be covered with an expensive Italian ceramic tile. But all ceramic tile work needs a solid backing to support itself. After discussing the profile of the tub with my best concrete form carpenter, I located a steel fabricator who fashioned a series of four round angle iron rings with small hole drilled in the ring about six inches apart. These rings would have ¼ inch plywood applied to the rings three layers thick. The plywood cones would then be suspended from above and held in place while the concrete was poured around the edges. It was very imaginative but worked out perfectly. When Larry saw the finished product he confiscated the angle iron rings to be used again and again for projects in the Denver area.

But I hadn't heard from Olive for over a week. It was too good to be true. Our painter was applying the last coat of enamel paint to the walls of the swimming pool when Olive walks in the building. Now remember how formal and conservative Olive is. She approaches me with this conversation. "I had a dream last night. I dreamt that I was standing in this pool area and from the whirlpool corner there was a fountain blowing bubbles around the room. They were floating all around the room. It was the most beautiful thing I have ever seen." I listened with a foreboding look on my face. Olive then continued talking," I stopped by the High School Art department and hired the art teacher to paint Blue-Colored bubbles, spraying across the walls just like I saw in my dream. He will be here in the morning to begin painting them!"

I was awe struck. I couldn't believe my own ears. An artist is coming to paint bubbles all over the swimming pool walls! Larry couldn't believe it either when I told him. But after listening and chuckling for a good ten minutes, he simply said, " If she wants bubbles, let her paint bubbles."

Sure enough, early the next morning this artist arrives to discuss his ideas and objective with me. After listening closely, I turn the pool area over to him for three days of 'Bubble Painting' In the back of my mind; I knew we could paint over the blue bubbles if they flopped. At the end of the three- day experiment, I walked through the finished project to inspect. Each bubble as they sprayed out of the Northwest corner was perfectly round in shape coming in a multitude of sizes. Each bubble was comprised of many shades of blue enamel paint with a soft white accent square set in just the right place to give the allusion of three dimensional bubbles. They were very well done and complimented the blue tile work of the swimming pool perfectly. I was impressed and Olive was totally fascinated when she saw the finished fountain. She even paraded a series of personal friends and relatives through the room over the next several days to get their opinions. It was a classic!

One of the unique features of this country club was the private dining room that was situated adjacent to the kitchen but on the opposite side from the public dining area.. The main dining room was designed more for the general public and the clientele of the golf course and could seat 50-60 people at a time. But the private dining room was much more formal. It was a long rectangular room with a maximum capacity of twenty-five. The center ceiling area of the room was recessed inside an alcove that extended the entire length of the room. And directly in the center of this alcove was a chandelier that hung down a couple of feet. The alcove itself was thirty-six inches wide by sixteen inches deep. Olive wanted the ceiling of the alcove covered in mirrors with the center mirror to have a sunburst etched into it. Amazing!

But the stickler was that a three-inch hole had to be cut in the middle of the sunburst to allow for the installation of the chandelier. Olive had contracted with a specialty glass shop in Denver to etch this masterpiece. The very first prototype was flown in using Frontier Airlines and arrived in six fractured pieces. Olive was devastated to say the least. She immediately called the shop in Denver and ordered a second sunburst. Then she called Glenn, her husband, and made arrangements for the company jet to pick up and deliver the second piece. This did a little better but still was shattered into four segments.

But Olive was not to be denied. A third sunburst mirror was ordered and my project manager in Denver was given the task of personally picking up the custom built crate and renting a new cargo van which he would personally drive the 500 miles to Cody. It finally made it in one piece and it did add immensely to the dramatic effect of that room. I don't even want to know what the final delivery bill was for the sunburst. WOW!

During the next couple of weeks, a rather disturbing wrinkle surfaced in regards to the Nielsens and the LDS church. The LDS stake center that was under construction in Cody was burned to the ground during the framing phase. The Nielsen's were concerned that it was related to their family's involvement over their years of service. Olive gave me a call that very day with a strange request. She wanted 24-hour security placed at the Country Club! She wanted guns there and a 'Big' dog to protect her pet project. I informed my office in Denver and promptly went to work.

The first person I thought of was my brother Chip with our Labrador retriever 'Flipper'. When I first asked him if he had any plans for the next couple of nights, I think he construed it as a ploy to keep him out of the bars. But when he accepted the fact that I really needed a night watchman at the Country Club, he readily accepted. I had him scheduled for a 12-hour shift. At six o'clock I left the building with Flip and Chip taking over his watch. I really had no idea of what to expect. The local police had set up a drive-by every hour or so with periodic inspections set up at random intervals.

I dropped by the Country Club around 11 P.M. to check in and drop off some 'Munchies' for both the dog and my brother. As I came walking around the corner of the swimming pool, Flip began howling as loud as I had ever heard him. I am sure he could be heard for miles around since the poolroom acted just like a megaphone. As soon as Flip recognized me however he came over for an ear scratch that I always gave him. Chip must have had a full box of 12 gauge shells near where he had his shotgun propped up. A cot and sleeping bag were decked out ready for the night. I did also notice an alarm clock sitting close by. I didn't expect Chip to stay awake for the entire shift. Flip would help in that department. The following morning I stopped by the police department to verify that nothing unusual had happened during the night. The security watch was called off after the Fire Investigator determined that an unhappy sub-contractor that hadn't been paid his retainage after completing his portion of the work set the church fire.

Towards the completion of the Olive/Glenn Country Club project, I received another unannounced visitor. This time it was from Glenn E Nielsen himself. He didn't live that far from the country club. As I approached him after he was noticed walking from room to room, he commented to me," I just thought I would stop by to see where all that money was being spent." He seemed pleased at the general appearance of the building itself. When he walked around the poolroom, I noticed a large grin on his face. He didn't comment on anything specific until we reached the kitchen. As he circled all the appliances in the state of the art kitchen, he turned to me and said," What this kitchen needs is a walk-in cooler." I looked a little confused because he motioned towards the back stairway and just said," It can hang over that stairway if nothing else." I was invited to come over to his home to see how his walk-in cooler was installed.

I arrived at the agreed upon time and rang the doorbell. I was definitely nervous meeting with the president of Husky Oil Company at his private residence. I recognized his son when the door opened. He escorted me towards the back of the huge home where Glenn was found tinkering in the kitchen. They chatted briefly and then he turned his attention towards me. He mentioned that he "wanted to have a little input in the final product of the Country Club." Where upon he headed towards a cooler that sat off to one side. As he stood there he just stated," I want you to relocate this cooler to the Country Club kitchen."

I just stood there staring at this modest sized walk-in cooler wondering if it was possible and where do I start? I grabbed my tape measure, which I had attached to my belt and took some preliminary measurements. My mind was racing at a million miles a second. I couldn't wait to get back and check out if it was at all feasible to relocate this cooler to the new kitchen at my project. On the way back to the project, I phoned Larry in Denver and explained what Glenn was requesting. All Larry said was," What will, they think of next?"

I took my dimensions and put what little design skills I had to work and began the process of remodeling. The area over the stairs would need to be used and the floor would need to be cantilevered out a couple of feet. The last modification was to frame in a new partition next to the standing refrigerators with a wall where the studs were installed on the flat. This would give me that additional two inches I needed to make everything fit. And finally after an additional two weeks of intense coordination, we had Glenn's walk-in cooler transferred to the new country club. The Olive/Glenn Country Club was completed. During my conversations with Glenn, he revealed his intention of donating the entire project to the City of Cody. Oh Well. What's four or five million when it involves the mega rich?

CHAPTER FOUR

MANAGER FOR TAGGART CONCRETE/ ROCKY MOUNTAIN PRE-MIX

During the last three weeks of work on the Country Club, I received daily visits from an old friend, Mac Taggart. His company owned several concrete production outlets. One of those was located in Riverton, Wyoming. Riverton is located in the central part of the state about two hundred miles south of Cody. The manager that had been running the operation in Riverton had been killed in a freak accident. Mac needed a manager to run his division in Riverton and he wanted me to fill that position. I really wanted to finish the project for the Nielsens before I moved my family to Riverton. But Mac was desperate, and we headed to River City just as soon as arrangements could be made.

Mac was aware that I had a house to sale in Cody. But he still wanted me to purchase the home of the widow there in Riverton. I had made several trips to Riverton to see the home and the business situation. The home was less than a year old and in good shape. But the business was hurting. The temporary manager and his assistant were stealing from the company. A manager was needed!

I accepted Mac's offer with a few conditions from both sides. Mac instructed me to dismiss the two guilty operators as soon as possible. He would make the arrangements for my family to move into the widow's home and I would start making the payments just as soon as my home in Cody sold. The company would pack up our belongings in Cody and deliver them to Riverton on Mac's ticket. A date was set and my family jumped into our Ford Maverick along with the new pickup that the company would furnish me.

I had informed the widow in Riverton of the arrangements and notified her of the date when we would arrive. Riverton was right in the middle of a uranium boom. It was practically impossible to find a decent home to rent or buy anywhere close to town. The home was the right size for us but it didn't have a blade of grass, a fence, or any vegetation. We arrived in Riverton full of anticipation and apprehension too. Riverton was just about the same size as Cody. It was located next to the Wind River Mountains and had a river running along the South side of town.

This river and the Owl Creek Mountains served as the northern boundary of the Wind River Indian Reservation, one of the largest Indian reservations in the United States. It had two tribes that shared the resources of this reservation. The Eastern Shoshone and the Northern Arapahoe lived on opposite sides of this government-regulated area. I was to learn a tremendous amount about each tribe and their peoples over the next twenty years.

The home we had been promised was part of a new subdivision on the Eastern side of town. As we drove up to the home, I noticed a lock box on the front door with an address noted on it for a contact. I knocked on the door and tried the doorbell several times. The home was empty. I asked around the businesses on that side of town to try and identify where the contact listed on the lockbox was located. We finally were successful. But upon discussing the situation with the attorney at that address, I was informed that the previous owner had returned to Nevada and was emphatic that the keys remain sealed until the earnest monies were deposited in a special account.

I was devastated to say the least. The widow had thrown our previous agreement out the window and was trying to get the equity in the home sent to her up front! I placed a call to my boss in Cody and explained the situation. He was flabbergasted as well. I told Mac that with those terms I would be forced to return to Cody and reject his employment offer. After some intense discussion on the phone, I agreed to find a hotel for three or four days while the whole thing could be sorted out.

We located the local Holiday Inn and were able to get a single night room for my family. It was a typical Holiday Inn and for whatever reason, we were only able to secure that room for one night only. The local Sundowner hotel was just across the street. We booked two rooms for the rest of the week. While Mac worked out the housing snafu, we began exploring Riverton.

We located the church and their grocery shopping facilities. A slow trip down main street and an up and back drive along Federal Blvd. and the extent of what stores Riverton had to offer had been located. I was sure they had a hospital but we didn't have too much luck finding it during that first day. We did see some nice city parks and some nice looking homes. We also could see a large agricultural area sprawling out to the East and West.

Mac made the arrangements with the widow and her attorney and we were able to get moved into the home after just a few days. It was nice but needed some cleaning and a fair amount of repairs. But we were official Rivertonites. We began the rough-in period. Getting to know our neighbors and members of the church in that community.

I had begun my new work assignment. I knew it was going to be an uphill battle but I wasn't totally ready for what I found. The concrete plant had five mixer trucks and four gravel-hauling trucks. The mechanic had quit the day before and the paper work was at least a month behind. I was also informed that the city had rejected over a thousand yards of curb and gutter that had recently been placed and the rolls on the small rock crusher at the pit needed to be replaced A.S.A.P. Now where to start in that quagmire? I forgot to mention that I had little to no experience in the production of specification sands and gravels let alone ready mixed concrete. Help!

Fremont County, Wyoming is huge and comprises oil field sites and uranium diggings along with the typical construction sites. Trying to cover a 100 square mile area would prove daunting, but to try and cover that same area with only five concrete mixers without radio communication is impossible. I voiced this concern time and time again. I was unable to convince the bookkeeper that it was imperative that I be able to talk to my drivers. How in the world was I to maintain any type of a schedule? I even took it upon myself to order a radio system for the plant and all our trucks. The head office refused to authorize the expenditure. I was told that my sales volume needed to double in order to justify that expense. So I set out to sell a thousand yards of concrete per month instead of the five hundred yards that had been the previous norm.

    I had to find a qualified mechanic to keep the fleet operational and quick! I was fortunate in that the big uranium companies were starting to downsize. I hired Martin on a part-time basis fully expecting him to quit as soon as he found full time employment with benefits. He was well qualified and quite orderly and proficient when it came to his repairs and maintenance logs. He was a keeper.

    I couldn't believe the monthly records had slipped as bad as they had. The part-time secretary was only able to complete the reports with the information she was given. The interim managers were totally ill prepared to handle that workload. They understood the day-to-day operations of the plant and the crusher. And that was what they devoted their time towards. As I watched them direct the work of satisfying orders and making deliveries on time, I knew that Mac was right on target. They had to be replaced as soon as possible.

    One of the first executive decisions I had to make was at the U S Energy Trailer Park. A thousand yards of curb and gutter had been rejected because of low compressive strengths. We had to remove the defective curb and gutter, correct the mix design, and re-pour the thousand yards of curb and gutter to the design standards of the City of Riverton. The removal was very simple. It was definitely inferior concrete. The gradation of the concrete aggregates, cement analysis and quantities, and mixer certifications were all verified. There was no reason that the mix supplied should have failed. The problem had to be in the handling of the product in the field after delivery.

The U S Energy employees themselves were placing the curb and gutter by means of a curb machine recently purchased. I watched the machine at work and noticed several oddities. The machine worked on the same principle of extrusion that most curb laying machines used. The concrete was poured into a hopper and then forced through a metal silhouette of the profile needed. But this particular machine did not use any vibration devices to consolidate the concrete. The concrete was of a very dry mixture so as to stand by itself immediately following the extrusion. There was also a hopper on the rear of the machine that delivered a cement slurry to the top of the curb and gutter giving it a very professional appearance. But the integral component of the product had not been consolidated and the remaining voids in the profile were what were causing the failures.

The slump of the concrete was critical. If it was too stiff, the consolidation did not happen. The machine would operate at peak speed thus achieving maximum efficiency of the men working behind the machine. If the concrete was too wet, the machine did not have any mass behind itself to propel itself forward. The concrete had a very narrow margin of acceptability to accomplish the designed product. I would spend the next ten days monitoring the delivery of every load of concrete to verify its consistency and conformity to standards. Following the replacement of the curb and gutter, I informed the people at U S Energy that we would no longer supply concrete to that particular machine until vibrators were installed to consolidate the concrete supplied. That would set off a chain of events that I would feel for the next two years.

The rock crusher we were using at our pit was commonly called a 'jaw and roll' crusher. The Jaw would crusher the 4 to 6 inch rocks into 2-inch rocks or smaller whereupon the Roll would pulverize the rocks down in size to one inch or smaller. It was small and very much out-of-date. Its output needed to be twice what it was in order to be cost effective. And it was down more than it was running. We needed an upgrade in the worst way.

All of these issues were thrust on a green apprentice from college. That would be me. I spent hours studying and reading everything I could get my hands on. Concrete production was much more demanding than I ever realized. The more I studied the more I realized that quality controls at Taggart Concrete were virtually non-existent. I began implementing steps to correct that deficiency. The crews didn't understand why. The men who accepted the changes were allowed to stay on staff. The crew that fought at their implementation was let go. It seems like I was hiring and firing men every other day. But slowly and surely we were improving the quality of the finished product.

And with that improvement in product, I was slowly increasing our sales from month to month. I lost count of the personal contacts I made to contractors and owners alike trying to convince them that our product was superior and since our prices were lower, we should be their first call. It would take the better part of fifteen years to become the top concrete producing company in Fremont County but I made it.

But I was becoming quite knowledgeable in some of the finer points of concrete quality control. One project that I vividly remember was at the Wyoming State Honor Farm. The minimum-security inmates of the State Penal system were housed just outside of Riverton. The contractor that was pouring the foundation for a new dormitory chose us to supply the mud. It was in the spring of that year and winter always brings a multitude of issues with it. This year was no exemption.

The footings were in place and a large wall pour was to take place on a Friday. The weekend would provide ample cure time for the concrete to achieve its design strength. The pour was finished and insulated tarps were placed over the forms to capture the heat generated during the hydration of the concrete.

Early that next Monday, I received a phone call from the project manager at the site. His voice was quite excited as he said," You have got to see this for yourself!" It was a short five-minute drive to the Honor Farm. He was right when he said I wouldn't believe what had happened. I walked over to the forms still in place and took a quick gander at the problem. The concrete supplied there last week was just sitting there. No hydration and taken place what so ever. The mix had not frozen since it was protected, but it was just as fluid as the moment it was placed. That is strange …very strange!

I called the batch plant to verify what mix design had been used. The same design used for the footings had been delivered. So I began an investigation into how the hydration of those 40 yards of concrete had been killed. My probing into what might have happened finally identified the use of a new barrel of Air Entrainment Admixture. (This admixture generates thousands and thousands of microscopic air bubbles into the concrete that helps it to withstand freezing temperatures) I discovered that if this mixture freezes before it is dispensed into the mixer truck, that it would totally kill the chemical reaction called hydration. We were guilty and needed to rectify the problem.

I had some friends that worked for the volunteer fire department. They would deliver a few hundred gallons of water in their pressurized truck. A couple of concrete forms would be removed from the wall pour and the pressurized water would then wash out the defective product. It worked slick as a whistle. We had several truckloads of slimy gravel to haul away, but the wall pour was readied again. This time using non-frozen admixtures, we had the project back on schedule. The profit that might have been realized from the contract was obviously non-existent. Another valuable lesson learned.

But if a concrete supply company wants to make money in Wyoming, they must learn how to handle the temperatures. We had landed a major contract in supplying the concrete for a ten thousand yard wastewater treatment plant project there in Riverton. One of the first pours scheduled was a continuous four hundred yard footing pour during the second week of January. It has been known to drop into the sub zero range temperature wise and remain there for weeks. The weather forecast was followed religiously. The goal was to be ready for any 24-hour period of above Zero temperatures. The forecast promised a 5-day Chinook that could be what we needed.

CONSTRUCTION HICCUPS

The contractor had a large concrete pump with a back up ready to go. A twenty five-man concrete crew was ready to man the continuous pour even if it took all night long. On the supply end, we had to be ready for just about anything. We had an over abundance of aggregates ready, three cement haulers ready to unload their powdery cargo into our silos, and an oil field hot water buffalo full loaded with a thousand gallons of hot water. All of these tricks learned would be needed during that extra long night. That with a small fleet of mixer trucks that had passed the State's rigid inspections was all ready.

We started the pour at eight A.M. on a Wednesday morning. Everything began on a smoothly planned schedule. But somebody invited Murphy to attend the pour. You know what Murphy's Law is all about. "Anything That Can Go Wrong, Will Go Wrong" The first issue was the concrete pump plugging after just 75 yards being placed. We added some plasticizers to help the mix during pumping. It worked well and we had plenty of plasticizer on hand.

The next mishap occurred when the trunk of the pump truck got hung up in the rebar double matt. That cost the crew another hour to rectify the problem. It was just like that hour after hour, one break down after another. The only bright spot in the whole ordeal was in our obligation to supply the specification product to the jobsite when called for. We rotated drivers and batch men throughout the night in order to satisfy the contract. I can still see in my mind's eye a dozen men draped over chairs, couches, and improvised beds in order to catch any sleep possible. But as soon as the phone alarm sounded, they would all jump back into action. Sunflower seeds and gallons of hot coffee were downed that night as we fulfilled our delivery contract to the 'T'!

Cold weather production is a given while working in Wyoming. But I also had occasion to battle the other extreme. We had a bridge deck that needed to be placed along the Dubois highway. It posed a couple of challenges. It was located approximately halfway between Dubois and Riverton. It was also located on the Wind River Indian Reservation.

The specifications called for a continuous deck pour of eight hundred yards of a 7-¼-sack mix. It was scheduled for a mid-July placement date. Both the contractor and the Highway Department, wanted to use a portable batch plant with all aggregates imported to the site. We were selected as the supplier. A computerized plant was scheduled to be located at the Bull Lake site. The specifications were very strict when it came to placement. The concrete temperature had to be below a certain degree in order to achieve the desired solution. I proposed the use of ice as the solution.

The concept had been utilized in Las Vegas many times. But in Wyoming it was unproven. We didn't have the machinery needed, let alone located 35 miles from town. But where there is a will, there is a way. I had made arrangements for the quantity of ice needed in Riverton. All I had to do was get it to the jobsite and then into the mix.

I located some heavy-duty insulated concrete blankets and a couple of day laborers. We loaded the bagged ice in one of our ten-yard end dumps, which had the insulated tarps as liners. This was loaded up around four A.M. in order to be at the jobsite at daybreak. Everything was going as planned.

That day was a perfect hot-weather concrete day. A cloud cover was present which helped lower the ambient temperature. The batch plant fired up just before the sun broke over the surrounding mountain peaks. The pour was progressing nicely. About ten o'clock the foreman decided that the ice was needed. We calculated the weight of the water removed from the batch weight. It would be replaced with an identical weight of ice. It worked to perfection. The laborers began dumping the bags of ice into the mixers at the same time as the batch water. (Of course the plastic bags were disposed of properly) The temperature of the concrete mix was lowered to an acceptable level and the pour was completed on schedule! Both the contractor and the Highway Engineer on-site were amazed at how easy the pour had been accomplished. If they only knew what had taken place during the pour and was kept hidden from probing eyes and ears.

CONSTRUCTION HICCUPS

That following summer, I was to benefit from some seeds I had planted months earlier. I had approached the City Engineer about doing some paving with concrete in lieu of asphalt. I had all but written the possibilities off as a fantasy. There were no contractors in the area that had neither the equipment nor the manpower to handle such work. But then completely out of the blue, a street-paving contract was advertised that had an alternate to use concrete instead of the black conventional method. But the cool thing about it was an out of town paving contractor was determined to secure the bid.

He had access to a Gomaco Paver that could place the street, curb and gutter, and the sidewalk all in one pass. And I mean from back of sidewalk to back of sidewalk! The total distance across was close to sixty feet total. When he approached me, he was skeptical that we could supply the 2000 cubic yards needed in a continuous pour. The other suppliers in the area had dismissed the project as being impossible. I looked at the total project as an enviable challenge. We struck up a deal and before we knew it the project was ours. Now all I had to do was convince my bosses.

I knew the capability of the batch plant. It could batch a truck every ten minutes. But could it sustain that cubic yard per minute rate for a twelve to thirteen hour span without any breakdowns? We would need ten concrete mixers to deliver the material allowing for a slim margin of error. And we would need stockpiles of two thousand yards of both fine and course aggregates. My cement silos only had the capacity for half that much, so a convoy of cement haulers would need to be hired out on a rigid schedule. We were lucky to have a canal close by and the water right to the water we needed. After days of brainstorming with my bosses, we had a plan in place.

That day started early for me, I didn't trust anybody else to man the batching duties. The pre-pour conference on the previous day had everybody assigned to a station with very specific duties. I would be sitting at the control panel with a state inspector watching my every move. Our crew was comprised of two loader operators, two spotters, ten mixer drivers, two men to man the pumps, and our mechanic complete with his total array of tools and equipment. The one unexpected item on the list was the two concrete mixer trucks that my boss hired from Casper. They were large ten-yard haulers and a bright yellow color. (The other trucks were all white)

That day was perfect. The weather cooperated. All the schedules meshed perfectly. The project was a total success. The only incident happened about half way through. Our mixer trucks were stacking up waiting to unload. The Gomaco Screed was being re-fueled and one of our drivers made an off-handed remark to the contractor. "Well, I guess we showed you guys how it's done!" The foreman turned to see how had made the remark. I big grin appeared across his face as he said," Do you see this lever pointing at the number One speed? Watch what happens when I set it on the number two!" That Gomaco Screed shifted into a higher gear and swallowed up the eight waiting trucks in as many minutes. I knew something had happened when all of a sudden we had eight trucks all returning to the plant right on top of each other! Contractors were talking about that pour for weeks afterwards.

But the concrete supply business isn't always a rosy scenario. I can remember one June afternoon when I received a frantic message from one of our mixers that needed help and fast! He either turned off his radio or who knows what happened but I totally lost all communication with him. I quickly checked his delivery ticket. He was suppose to be delivering rock in a mixer truck some thirty miles west of town down by the river. I jumped into my pickup and made a beeline to the intended location. I couldn't help but envision the worst as I sped along the highway. Was he in the river? Was he just lost? What in the world would I find when I got there?

Nothing could have prepared me for what I found. After I dropped off the highway towards the river, I came upon the following scene. The mixer was facing towards town so his load had probably been delivered. But there he was standing on the edge of a wooden bridge with his mixer truck pointing straight up in the air! He had crossed the bridge once, but on the return trip across the bridge, it collapsed from underneath his truck as the rear axles crossed over. Nobody was hurt, but what in the world was I going to do now?

We could see a portion of the highway from where the accident had occurred. And as I stood there scratching my head in confusion, my driver yells out," there is a crane coming down the highway and its headed our way!" I couldn't believe my own eyes. A crane of just the right size to handle the load and at just the right time! I quickly drove to intercept them and within minutes I had a 30-ton crane resting near the nose of that concrete truck. The crane operator was in total amazement as to the predicament we were in and to the lack of damage to the mixer truck. The crane was able to secure a cable to the rear end of the truck. And with the truck in Neutral, the crane hoisted the load up in the air enough to roll the entire truck far enough away from the bridge to safety. The driver jumped into the cab, fired up the engine, and headed for home. No damage to the drum or nothing. After we finally reached the plant, our mechanic gave the truck a good once over inspection, while I proceeded to give my driver a good once over butt chewing on what he had done wrong!

Over the years, I found myself in many unusual situations. I would be called to extract three full-loaded mixer trucks from a field of slime, I would lose a mixer full of concrete to a blown engine, and I would run my arm around a head conveyor drum while trying to clean it during operations. I had learned both the pros and the cons about the construction supply business. But I still felt the need to get more involved with the contractors themselves. I wanted to be a contractor.

My chance came when I decided to build my own home. I had solicited bids from my clientele. But when they all came in over budget, I moved to be my own general contractor. I received a bonus that year in the form of a two-acre piece of ground near the batch plant. I had no idea what chain of events lay in store for me during that summer.

I drew up the plans for a passive solar designed home. There wouldn't be any solar panels but the sun would be used to partially heat the home by warming concrete and masonry mass, which in turn would radiate that warmth back into the home after the sun had disappeared. I also utilized earth-berming to help insulate the during the winter months. It would prove educational and cost effective.

I hired a local excavator to dig the soil prior to setting forms for the foundation. I was totally surprised when the desired depth had been achieved and not a single solitary rock was encountered. The sandiest soil I had ever seen was encountered all the way down twelve feet. I was concerned. A good friend inspected the undisturbed soils at the bottom of the excavation and gave his engineered opinion," Looks just fine to me!" But I was still apprehensive.

In discussing the situation with my boss, who was also an engineer. He suggested that wider footing dimensions might give me the piece of mind I was looking for. And since the concrete I was using was being supplied at cost, I tripled the width of the footers. I can still remember that first concrete pour. The wind was blowing rather briskly and it seemed like every grain of sand that could possibly blow into my hair, eyes, and ears did so. But the footers and walls were poured, all using the dimension lumber from the framing package to be used latter on. The only lumber lost during the process came when the bank caved way during the wall pour. The mixer backed in a foot closer than it should have. I should have taken a picture. The rear tires of the truck were hanging out in free space while the rest supported the remaining weight. I had dodged a bullet to say the least.

The next step was to pour the basement floor. I was promoting a product at the plant called 'Flowable Concrete'. The same proportions of cement, aggregates, and water were used. But the water-reducing agents were doubled. This yielded a concrete mix that was considerably easier to handle. I found out that the hydration time was at least twice as long. My driver and I poured the slab around 4 O'clock in the afternoon. It was a warm day in June and typically the finishing operation would have been complete by at least 10 P.M.

But I was to learn first hand about the side effect of 'Flowable Concrete'. I was still hand finishing that slab at 2 A.M. that next morning! I received a visitor, as I was totally preoccupied in my project. My wife had sent a county sheriff out to the jobsite to see what was taking me so long. She didn't want to haul our four children out in the middle of the night. I was just fine and the concrete did finally set so I could trowel the surface to my satisfaction.

My children were very excited to be getting a new home. So much so, that I looked for ways they could help. After setting the floor joists, I laid out the ¾ inch floor sheathing just like it was needed. I tacked the plywood down at each corner. I then snapped red chalk lines over the floor joists. I had procured fifty pounds of 8d nails along with four small hammers. I turned the kids loose on the sub-floor with instructions to hammer a nail along the red lines every 4-6 inches apart. And away they went!

I should have anticipated that things wouldn't go as smooth as I wanted. I received a phone call a short time later that they were out of nails and needed more. Fifty pounds of nails should have been more than enough to complete the task. What were they doing with all those nails? When I arrived, the scene was a classic. Some of the nails were only 1-2 inches apart and then it seemed like the chalk line had disappeared. The nail lines diverged into various unforeseen angles and paths. After a good chuckle and some new lines were snapped, the task was completed. That subfloor wasn't going anywhere, even in the strongest Wyoming Wind!

My Passive Solar design relied on the sun heating the building materials during the day and then releasing that warmth back into the home at night. I worked with concrete block in the main portion of the living quarters. I knew that additional heat would be needed. I had two wood burning stoves incorporated into my design. Each stove would be lined with firebrick. This would allow me to burn coal as well as wood. Wyoming is well known as a coal producing state. My plan was perfect except for one small detail. The banks would not lend me the monies needed without a conventional heat source. So I included some electric baseboard heaters into the overall scheme of things.

At that time, the Federal Government was very interested in energy conservation. A program was in place that would refund upwards of twenty per cent for the installation of energy conserving items during new construction. I located some ultra efficient windows that also had insulating louvers inside the double panes of glass. I could install these windows and recoup a huge amount of the extra costs when I filed my tax returns. BINGO!

So I began framing, making as few withdrawals from my construction loan as possible. But leave it to the Feds to gum up the works. No sooner had I begun drawing monies as needed, I was informed that the program I was building under could only guarantee the loan for six months! So what had started out, as a part time indulgency now was the most intense undertaking of my life. Every spare minute I had was spent working on the house. I recruited a couple of my brothers to help out as well. The pressure was immense and quite a few corners were cut so as to achieve my date. But we did it! (We actually moved in to the house before we had running water) But we did it!

I can still see my brother, Chip, on the roof laying shingles while I concentrated on the siding. My other bother, Ron, spent hours grading the lawn areas to achieve the drainage needed away from the house. My wife along with some friends painted and wallpapered the interior walls just ahead of the floor coverings. And multiple friends helped with cabinetry, tile work, and the last minute details. We now had a home filled with memories.

We decided to hold a huge house warming to commemorate the occasion. A barbeque complete with homemade root beer and all the fixings! There were at least fifty people invited. We also invited my immediate family over for Christmas that year. Now that was a gathering of gatherings. Fourteen families sleeping and eating under a single roof is no small feat. We were fortunate however; the winter snows were late that year, allowing us to entertain outdoors. We had a horseshoe tournament between Christmas and New Years. (I think my brother, John, and my Dad went home with the bragging rights)

There is always some extra items that needed to be completed after we had moved into the house. My front driveway was one of those items. As the manager of the Pre-Mix plant, I had access to some advantages not normally available. The use of their front-end loader from time to time and extra concrete that was not used completely by the customers. I always had a section of the driveway formed just in case a partial load needed a place to call home. It always was a stretch to get the concrete in place and finished properly before my duties forced me to return to the plant. I can remember one of those hot summer days very vividly.

I had a large load rejected for some small reason and after sending another batch to the waiting customer, I ran to my house to place the waiting concrete. I was able to get it down and finished before the phone rang again. So I hopped into my pickup and scooted back to the batch plant. My youngest daughter, Karen, had been keeping an eye on our Labrador pup during the concrete pour in front of the garage. Upon seeing me leave, she decided that the job was complete. She hopped on to her tricycle and proceeded to make a dozen loops through the still slightly wet concrete. Our dog couldn't resist the excitement and began chasing behind her barking and enjoying the feel of fresh concrete under his paws! Jeanette came out to see what all the barking was about, but it was too late. The dog prints, the tricycle tracks, and Jeanette's attempt to repair the damage with the cement trowel can still be seen to this day in front of the garage doors!

CHAPTER FIVE

SKYLINE CONSTRUCTION

While I was building my home, I had developed a pretty good relationship with many of the contractors and suppliers in the area. Many of them wanted a good reliable concrete sub-contractor that did good work and was not so expensive. I had discussed this with my boss in Lander. He was not very receptive. He felt like we would be in direct competition with most of the clientele that he had cultivated over the years. He knew the Lander side of the market. But I had developed the Riverton side, and it needed a better grade of contractor.

So I started bidding on small projects around the area, which I felt would not have any conflict of interest with our base of customers. I planned on using the base of contractors in the Riverton area to satisfy these contracts. I landed several contracts outside the county. But in so doing, some of my earlier competitors surfaced. They felt like I was trying to take over the entire concrete market. That was the furthest thing from my mind. I could never grow that big nor did I want to. But the die was cast!

I decided to open up my own contracting company. Skyline Construction was organized and off and running. I discussed it with my wife and she was ready or so we thought. I had worked with a sub in town that was selling out. He had a reasonable amount of equipment and the price was right. But that is where the rub began. What little savings we had was gobbled up in a heartbeat. The 2-ton truck that came with the deal refused to cooperate. I had to jump start it every morning and that was using our family car. I had two contracts that required my every skill. A BLM contract in Guernsey, which is, located some 200 miles Southeast from Riverton. I had good money in the bid but I didn't have a crew to form and pour the base for the cell tower that would follow.

I hired a couple of high school kids and we loaded up the 2-ton with forms, rebar, tools, and a fresh new battery for a couple of days at Guernsey State Park. The first day was spent locating the jobsite, which took half the day. It was right out in the open flats with nothing surrounding us except sagebrush. Then why was it so hard to find? I had a simple map sketched on the back of a year old calendar and two hundred square miles of Wyoming Sage to search. NO PROBLEM!

But find it we did. And we crammed eight hours of work into six. It was dark and we unrolled our sleeping bags at the closest campsite we could find. I had called the local concrete supplier and arranged for three mixers to deliver the 6-bag mix starting at 7 A.M. with trucks to arrive every half hour apart. We roasted a couple of Brats each and hit the hay.

I rousted my helpers out early since I wanted to be at the site by 6:30 A.M. to be ready for the first delivery. We munched on some cold milk and doughnuts on the way to the designated site. The BLM Inspector assigned to oversee the placing of the concrete was at the locked gate exactly when he said he would be there. But as we drove through the gate, we turned to see what was making all the dust on the road we had just come down. Lo and behold, we could make out the silhouette of a concrete truck approaching. But wait, it had two mixers following right behind it. The supplier had taken it upon himself to send all three trucks together instead of staggering them as we had agreed. I was in trouble right out of the chute as they call it in the rodeo circle.

My inspector had a slight smirk on his face. And I had panic in my eyes. But with a deep breath, I began barking orders. The extra two mixer drivers were told to put their drums in slow mix mode. I put them to shoveling and raking the four-inch slump concrete into place. The first load went down smoothly probably because I made sure it didn't touch any of the forms. But as I began laying the next truckload around the perimeter, I could see the forms bulging ever so slightly. I stopped filling the forms all the way to the top and opted to only lay the concrete halfway up the forms.

This seemed to have solved the bulging form problem. That is until the vibrator was plunged into the fresh mud. The bulging problem came rushing back but this time with twice the impact. I jerked the vibrator out away from the perimeter and used it sparingly in the center section. The perimeter was hand massaged using a rubber mallet instead. Every once in a while I would glance at my inspector. He was busy making notes on his clipboard after taking numerous pictures of the progress. But finally we had the 24 yards of concrete down and screeded. I was totally spent.

But I received my second wind and after a thirty-minute reprieve, we continued with the finishing operations. The edges were hand floated by the two green hands after I showed them the correct method I wanted followed. I positioned my power trowel on the far side of the pour and filled it with fresh gasoline. At just the right time, we placed the trowel onto the slab. With a strong pull on the starter cord the engine roared to life. I grabbed the handles and began the slow methodical floating of the entire slab. My green hands kept working the edges as I had shown them. They also began the cleaning of our cement tools and loading of the screed boards into the truck. I kept a close eye on the surface as I crisscrossed the slab. Every once in a while I stole a glance over to the BLM inspector and wondering when he was ever going to leave. But he was there for the long haul.

I had completed my final pass of the surface and we pulled the trowel off the slab. A few quick passes by hand and the trowel marks left by the machine were gone. I had my companions load the machine into the 2-ton, while I was discussing the day's work with the inspector. Over all, he was pleased with the surface and the flatness of the slab. He did offer a couple of pointers however. He was convinced I knew what I was doing, but he suggested that I hire some different help for the future. He was pleasantly surprised that we had salvaged the pour after he saw all the concrete arrive at the same time.

He rated us as a B+ contractor. We had room for improvement. I couldn't argue that point at all. We loaded up everything and headed back to Riverton.

I was definitely under high stress. My savings were gone, my cash flow was being stretched to the max, and I was beginning to doubt my abilities as a manager and a contractor. My better half knew that I needed a moment to regain my equilibrium. She loaded up all our camping gear and the whole family headed to the Sunlight Basin. Jeanette didn't really like the Sunlight country because of the bear stories she had heard from the area. But she knew I loved the sites and sounds associated with Sunlight Creek in the late summer. She knew me better than I knew myself. Even with the frustrations I was feeling, she knew I was qualified to undertake any construction project. The money problems would work themselves out. That short chance to catch my breath was all that I needed. My next contract was ready when we returned to Riverton.

WYOMING STATE TRAINING SCHOOL CHAPEL

I was contracted by Wilkinson Construction to complete the concrete work for a new Chapel at the State Training School in Lander. I would get to know Layne first as a Superintendent and later as an employee. The Chapel that we would build was a combination remodel/new construction to be located at the grounds located on the East side of Lander. I was intrigued with it, since several portions of the building would be relocated from a chapel in Cheyenne some 300 miles away.

Up unto that point, I really didn't understand what the Training School was all about. Apparently the Sate of Wyoming receives Federal monies to house and 'train' young people who have suffered head injuries and/or birth defects that affect their brain functions. My whole crew had to be vetted by the authorities in charge before they could work within this managed facility. We were placed under a very specific set of rules while on the premises.

These rules came into play during that first week in Lander. We liked to start as early as possible in order to take advantage of the cooler morning temperatures. But that particular morning we were escorted from the front gate to the Security Offices. We hadn't been given a reason and consequently we became very curious. Finally we were ushered into their Quiet Room. We were informed that there had been an Issue during the early morning hours. One of the residents had left his room without notification and had climbed onto the roof of the tallest building in the facility. He could be seen sitting on top of the roof, which reached three stories high! And nobody had been able to talk him down. They explained that a ladder truck from the local Fire Department was in route and that the issue should be resolved within the hour. We had a ringside seat for the extraction.

The ladder truck was put into location and two firefighters quickly climbed onto the roof. We couldn't hear anything that was being discussed but could definitely see the resident shaking his head back and forth rather vigorously several times. I then watched as one of the firefighters removed his helmet and held it in front of the belligerent resident. It was an offer we were to find out. The resident would be given a helmet if he would climb down with them to safety. It was a DEAL! And after a two-hour stand off, the resident climbed down the ladder on his own and waited for the helmet at the bottom of the ladder.

A deal was a deal. The firefighter turned to the rescued fellow and handed him his helmet. He promptly placed it on his head even though it was too big and began strutting around like he was King for the Day. The whole incident was the talk of the school for days to come. And we actually saw the resident modeling his new attire several more times for his friends to see. But we were put on strict compliance with our tools and especially our hard hats, in order to detour any future incidents.

But a short time later, we were all given a treat. The Training School had a tradition for Halloween. All of the residents and the workers on duty would dress up in their Halloween costumes for the day. And during their lunch hour, a full-blown parade was formed and sent around the entire Training School grounds. We were not allowed to participate, thank heaven, or I would have had several of my employees dressed up in their scariest getups imaginable leading the parade! They will have to wait for their treats back home like everybody else.

Another twist happened on that job that I was not expecting at all. I needed some trained employees and couldn't locate any. One of the guards at the Training School mentioned to me in passing that the Honor Farm in Riverton might be able to help supply the qualified help I needed. The inmates at the Honor Farm were in fact prisoners of the State but since they were guilty of minor offenses, they could become eligible for a work release program. I knew the Warden over at the Honor Farm so I decided to check into the possibility. I checked into the program and was surprised that a journeyman cement finisher was in fact part of that experiment.

I made arrangements to give Darrell a try. I picked him up that following Monday in Riverton. I had a good 30-minute interview with him on our way to Lander. I found out that he was from Torrington and he was serving time for Grand Theft and destruction of Private Property. He told me the whole story. He was working for a contractor near Laramie and had an argument with the foreman over wages. He had then hijacked one of their D-8 Bulldozers and proceeded to drive it right straight through the middle of the foreman's office trailer! He knew the man was not inside but he was convicted and sentenced for that event and had less than a year left on his term.

As I watched him work, I knew after just a short time that he was a keeper. I contacted the Warden in Riverton again and the final arrangements were put in place. But what happened next totally through me for a loop. Darrell informed me that he had his own transportation and I could arrange for him to drive to Lander every day by himself. I was dumbfounded but agreed to the arrangement. But the following day was a classic.

Ten minutes before starting time, Darrell drives on to the construction site in a bright red shiny Dodge Ram ½ ton pickup! I noticed right off the bat that the Dodge had Torrington license plates. What was going to happen next? Darrell parked the hand polished truck next to mine and went straight to work. During our first lunch break, he explained the whole policy about inmate use of personal vehicles to all the crew. He even bragged about the hand polished wax job. Apparently the rest of the inmates he housed with at the Honor Farm took pride in the fact that their dorm had the truck. And practically every night, they all would wash and wax the red shiny truck just to show it off a little.

Darrell was a willing and capable finisher. We had just begun placing and finishing the main concrete slabs for the new chapel. He wasn't afraid of hard work and even presented a few techniques on the use of inside screeds that we readily implemented. The concrete work was nearing completion and I was quite pleased with the final project. I didn't have another contract pending so I hired on with the Wilkinson crew for the winter. Darrell went back to the Honor Farm and the rest of my employees returned to school.

The next phase in the Chapel construction was to erect the massive Glu- Lam beams that would support the walls and the roof itself. There were a total of sixteen pairs of beams that would rest on the walls we had poured and butt up to each other high above the main floor. A large crane was employed to erect each beam. The operator was somewhat green because the very first beam he tried to slide into place was dropped! Layne was beside himself. The owner was brought in along with their insurance adjuster to remedy the solution.

The beams had been produced in Livingston, Montana. The beam was totally ruined and needed to be replaced. The plant in Montana was put on their RUSH time frame to replace the damaged beam. And I was sent to Livingston to pick up the beam with Wilkinson's 30-foot trailer. I was excited to actually see the plant and observe the process used to fabricate Glu-Lam Beams.

CONSTRUCTION HICCUPS

I was a little disappointed when I arrived at the Glu-Lam plant because our replacement beam had already been cut, glued, and planed to our specifications. But I was given an in-depth tour during the fabrication of another set of beams. I had expected an elaborate computerized plant equipped with the latest techniques available for the fabrication of Architectural Grade beams. What I found was a very simplistic approach to the whole process.

The lumber grades to be used were hand selected by a crusty old worker who had a laser mentality he had developed over many years of experience. The pieces of rough lumber were heated using a large steam tunnel. As they passed along the conveyors after being heat treated, a layer of industrial glue was applied to both sides. While the wood was still pliable and the glue workable, the lumber was placed in a press. The press was simply a series of solid steel posts slid into sleeves that had been anchored periodically using massive amounts of concrete. The clamps themselves were just large diameter pieces of all-thread shafts that had over-sized hex head nuts in place to ratchet down to the desired location. Air operated impact guns were then used to screw down the clamps to the design depth.

Once the glue was set and the wood had returned to its ambient temperature, the beams were run through a series of carbide-surfaced planers. These would shape and smooth the beam to the design specifications. An Inspector would then stamp and approve the finished product for shipment. The whole process was much more labor intensive than I expected but never the less quite efficient.

I delivered the beam back to Lander. The erection crew had set all but the last two beams while I was in Montana. And with this last beam, the structure could now be completed. The masons were infilling the outside walls with a split face block that was quite beautiful as it complimented the reds and browns of the beams. The next step was the installation of the stain glass mural that was in route from Cheyenne.

It arrived in Lander right on schedule. A glass-setting specialist had been hired by the State of Wyoming to remove, transport, and glaze the panels at their new home in Lander. The process was quite intriguing to say the least. Layne and I were stationed as assistants for the entire week. Any carpentry work we could do for the specialist was top priority. The trade of Glazing is a dying art all by itself. There are time restraints as well as special techniques used that separate the novice from the journeyman. All I learned in watching the process was to stay as far away from it as possible and leave it to the older craftsman. But the finished product was a jewel in our crown!

That next summer was consumed in concrete foundations and flatwork projects of all shapes and sizes. I did some architectural curbing and retaining walls for people that I knew. With many of them requiring imaginative formwork that I had never used before. The clients were very surprised that concrete could be used in such different ways and colors. I was also bidding on larger projects that required a larger crew. We poured foundations for the Highway Department and several schools in the area. I had set a restriction on my bids in that I would not work on a project over 100 miles from home. In Wyoming, that really limits the scope of your abilities. But I was committed to coming home every night, and not be away from home anymore than I had to.

As I worked around the county, I was always on the look out for good qualified hands that knew their way around a concrete pour. Formwork was easily taught to willing carpenters but then again there was flatwork. The setting of grade stakes, working with wet screeds, and hand-troweling was a skill set that was hard to teach and practically impossible to find close by. And any time I worked beside a journeyman finisher, I jumped at the chance to hire them. That is how I got to know Jerry and Wade.

I was hired out as a finisher on a large slab in Lander. The contractor knew I owned two power trowels, a 36-inch Thomas and a heavier 48-inch Kohler. He supplied four good hands and I supplied the a couple more helpers and the equipment. At that time I was using a 25-foot Gamaco power screed that I had purchased earlier. It was a beast of a machine and since it was a steel screed it took every bit of four men to move it around. But once it was set up it laid down a beautiful slab, as it was hand cranked along the surface.

Jerry and his buddies had never worked behind a power screed before but once they saw it in action they were hooked. It easily took the place of six well-trained concrete workers. As we completed that two hundred square foot slab, I approached Jerry with an offer to join me for the rest of the summer. He readily accepted.

They quickly learned my system of building formwork. They had experience using the Gates System as well as the Symons forms, which are great for standard box foundations. But my system of job built forms was much more flexible. Intricate shapes and designs were attainable and could be had for just a few dollars more. As I taught them about the how's and the why's, they picked it up quickly.

BOYSEN BOAT RAMPS

I had numerous bids out in an effort to meet all my financial obligations. The one bid that summer I did not think a legitimate possibility was for the construction of some boat ramps for the State of Wyoming's Parks Department. In the first place, the waters of the local Wind River Drainage were at an all time record low. And I had been informed by the State that several of my successful bids for concrete work were being tabled due to a shortage of funds. But my thinking was completely opposite to those who grant successful bidders. The low water conditions of the Boysen Reservoir mad it a perfect time to complete the boat ramps since pumping of the lake water was not a possibility.

In fact, it was somewhat of an embarrassment. There we were building a boat ramp that was 300 feet above the water line. The locals didn't see the lake ever getting to its normal levels in the near future. But we had the contract, and the money was good. As so often happens in the construction field, when one job begins another two or three surface at the same time. I found myself in that predicament again. So I placed Jerry in charge of the Boysen Boat Ramp while I tried to keep up with the remaining contracts.

Jerry and his buddies agreed to man the project. But when he decided to set his travel trailer on site, I should have baulked. It was about 80 miles from Lander to Boysen and could easily have been driven on a daily basis. Jerry's ploy was not to finish the job sooner but to take a vacation instead of work. They started out just fine but I received a few phone calls towards the end of the project that upset me severely.

I gave Jerry the benefit of the doubt and scheduled a surprise visit within the week. As I drove onto the jobsite, I could see my employees making a mad scramble to cover items inside their trailer. As I walked up to Jerry, I didn't need to be much of a detective to know that they had been drinking and drinking heavily. Jerry's face was as white as a sheet as I asked him fro an explanation. He him hawed around about why alcohol was on my construction sites in direct violation to my company policies and the policies of the State of Wyoming. After a feeble attempt to explain himself, I fired him on the spot!

That would really put me in a pickle. I still had the contracts to fill but now I was down a whole crew. I did the only thing I could do. I began burning the candle at both ends. I usually begin my days before daylight but now I continued working until well past sunset. I figured it would take me another two to three weeks to finish the ramps and then I could go back to my standard ten-hour day.

But the one thing I did enjoy about the new arrangement was the chances to put a RAKE finish to those ramps. The inspector was emphatic that the steep slopes of the ramps could not be too slippery to drive up. Usually the lighter the finish the better was used around town and for most customers. But a special TINED rake was purchased to apply the texture needed. The rake's 4 inch steel tines were flexible and spaced about a half inch apart. The trick was to pull that rake across the surface at just the right time. If it was too soon then the rocks in the concrete mix were dislodged leaving an almost mountainous effect. And if the surface was left too long then the coarseness of the surface was too smooth for the inspector. As we placed the slab, the inspector was practically standing on the ramp itself. He was going to make sure it was just the way he wanted it. But after several preliminary passes with the concrete tined rake, the inspector was satisfied. I would get to use that tined rake again in the foreseeable future, like I had a choice now that I was best buds with the local State inspector.

WESTERN NUCLEAR ACID PLANT EXPANSION

Shortly following the boat ramp incident, I was contracted by Don McClellan to form and pour a 65-foot diameter tank base at the neighboring Acid Plant. The story behind the plant is intriguing to say the least. Shortly after the uranium boom began in Fremont County, a decision was made to process the ore at the source instead of hauling it 60 miles for processing. The decision was a very sound decision based entirely upon the economics of the business.

The source of the uranium rich ore was located sixty miles East of Riverton. It was commonly called the Gas Hills probably because of earlier natural gas discoveries. Several mines were opened in this region and the small town of Jeffrey City sprung up over night. The mining unions had their fingers in the pie from the get go. Hundreds of operators and support staff were employed at these mines and they all were paid top union wages! The whole county was caught up in this uranium boom. Men were flocking into town by the thousands along with their families. Prices for just about anything skyrocketed. Housing was at a premium.

The mill located just South of Riverton was dismantled almost in its entirety and transported to the Gas Hills. The plant was converted to a nuclear acid producing facility. And near the end of the boom, it was decided that the tailings left at the Acid Plant were contaminating the Wind River drainage. A contract was let and all the tailings from that original processing site had to be hauled back out to the source. Over 100,000 cubic yards of radioactive tailings were transported back to the Gas Hills where they had been mined. At the end of this hauling contract it was decided to enlarge the Acid Plant itself. That is where I became involved.

Don McClellan had some steel 24-inch concrete panels and he devised a system of wooden beveled in fills that when installed between the panels formed the graduated spacers needed to provide the formwork for a round diameter wall twelve inches thick. I supplied the manpower and the tools necessary to complete this first tank. It went together quite nicely and well ahead of schedule. This allowed me to get my foot in the door so to speak for more tank bases. The most intricate of them was a small 25-foot diameter base with parallel support walls crossing the tank base every four feet.

The forming system that had been used for the larger tank base would not work for the smaller diameter. Again my site built forming system was ideal for the application needed. I typically use ¾ inch form-ply as the walls for our foundations. But I needed a small round diameter product. I contrived a layered system using three layers of ¼ inch plywood. The ¼ inch plywood could be forced into a circular pattern where the heavier plywood could not. It took some patience but we did achieve another masterpiece. The plant manager was equally impressed. So much so that he contracted with me to provide the concrete work for their new plant expansion.

It would involve a whopping 1500 cubic yards of concrete along with the entire earthwork related to it. The scope would last for the next sixteen months. I was always looking for winter work and this was my golden ticket. I approached Major's Equipment and signed a subcontract agreement with then to complete the digging and importing of suitable fill materials. As I was negotiating with the plant manager, he insisted that I include a round trip airfare to Florida. Western Nuclear was the parent company that owned the plant and they insisted that I sign the contract in person in Florida.

I had put that little detail far away in the back of my mind. I had some smaller projects to complete prior to the Acid Plant's anticipated ground breaking. And then out of the blue I get a phone call from Florida. I had a ticket to Orlando waiting for me in the

Riverton airport to leave at 9 A.M. I rushed home to gather up some things and tell my wife. She had been called to substitute at school. She wouldn't be available until after lunch. So with a small carry on and the details of my contract I walk on to that plane in Riverton. And after a layover in Denver and Dallas, I find myself in Orlando by 6 P.M.

The first thing I did was call home. I had left a short note on the counter before I had jumped on that plane. Jeanette was a little upset about the suddenness of the flight. She knew it was coming but did not anticipate the spontaneity of the whole thing. I had a meeting at their corporate headquarters in the morning and then a return flight home. Crazy as it all seemed, it was what I knew would happen in the back of my mind.

The taxi cab driver knew right where to take me. I arrived a few minutes early for my scheduled signing. As I sat there wondering what in the world I had gotten myself into, the regional construction manager and his assistant walk up to meet me. I was surprised that they had Western accents. But come to find out they were both from Montana of all places. We talked more about Billings, Montana than about anything else. And after our twenty- minute chat, they handed me a fully executed contract for the work back in Riverton. Apparently they had seen all that they wanted to see. We had not discussed one thing about the work that needed to be finished in the next year. They would let the manager in Riverton know that I was an individual that could be trusted and that I would do whatever it took to complete the job on time!

I had four hours until my return flight was scheduled to leave Orlando. I decided to rent a car and see some of the sights. I was totally blown away by the humidity and the smells in and around the gulf. I wanted to see some alligators of all things. So after getting some directions from the rental outfit, I headed towards an alligator farm just north of where I was. To say Florida is a little different than Wyoming is an understatement. That same old feeling I had experienced in South America had returned. Without any mountains for bearings, I was clueless which way was North or South. So I drove the safe route, which is I drove not turning off that highway for anything in fear off not being able to find my way back.

I did see an alligator however. As I was driving along in the right lane of that highway, I spotted a couple of logs laying at the edge of the borrow pit. As I approached them with my car they quickly spun around and dove back into the water that was standing at the bottom of the ditch. I glanced at my watch and quickly decided to leave Florida to the Floridians. I took a quick exit and headed back to the airport. I felt more comfortable spending the next two hours staring at the flight departure schedule than driving along a highway to who knows where. I am just a country boy from Wyoming and I couldn't wait to get back.

The Riverton Airport is very small but it sure was good to set foot on sound Wyoming soils again. Within a twenty- four- hour period, I had confirmed to me again that this is where I needed to be, in spite of all the difficulties. I promptly began hiring the necessary hands I would need to complete the Acid Plant Expansion. Since I would be working closely with Major's Equipment, I hired Jose who had worked with them for years. I also hired my brother, Ron, who was off for the summer. He was studying Civil Engineering at Utah State. If he could take a summer of concrete work he might just be good engineering material. I also hired a local schoolteacher that I had known for several years. Little did I know that Willie would go on to become one of my most reliable hands over the next several years?

The project kicked off with a formal ground breaking and everything. That was the first exposure I had with the 'Golden' shovel. The only difference between the 'Golden' shovel and any other new shovel was a can of Gold metallic spray paint. But we did have a brief ceremony to begin the project. And then on the very first day of construction, we hit water! And not just a little water show, but a full blown underground lake! We documented the problem and began the process of our first change order. It would eventually take four 2-inch submersible pumps located at each corner of the excavation to handle the flow of water generated.

The weight of the acid product was a determining factor in the design of the foundation. Acid weighs almost twice as much as water does! The volume that would be processed was astronomical. The design called for 24- inch structural slab supporting a 24-inch thick structural floor. The reinforcement was unbelievable. Number 7 rebar (7/8 inch diameter) on twelve inch centers with a double matt required in both slabs. There was hardly enough room for the concrete to penetrate the rebar mattes. Mechanical vibration was essential and I purchased two new vibrators for the job. But once the slabs were poured the dewatering requirement was completed. We were above the water table!

The design of the building was comprised of a concrete slab surrounded by concrete walls. Wood studs and sheetrock were not incorporated into the building at all because of the corrosive nature of all the products that were produced and handled. Even the piping was specific to anti-corrosive MONDI plastic pipe that would handle acid and at a third of the cost over Stainless Steel pipe. The concrete walls all had to be ground smooth and then sacked with a non-shrink rubbing compound to help it against the corrosion possibilities. The entire project was very specialized compared to conventional construction practices.

The entire summer was spent forming, grinding, and sacking concrete surfaces. My brother, Ron, definitely saw his share of work that summer. But one of his goals while spending the summer in Riverton was to stay in shape physically for the baseball scholarship he had waiting for him in Cedar City. The legs and upper body received more than enough exertion doing daily concrete work but his wind needed the conditioning too. I can still remember him challenging my young children to a race.

They could use their bicycles and he would race on foot. Our lane to our house was about a hundred yards long. He would challenge them to race up and back from the house. On the proper signal Ron would take off running at top speed and in his work boots as well. By the time he reached the end of the gravel driveway, the kids on their bikes had caught up to him. But they both had to change direction.

Ron would gain enough advantage in this direction change to insure his victory over the bicycles day in and day out!

But as if all that physical conditioning wasn't enough, Ron would always find time to take his nieces and nephew to the local swimming pool. He claims to have spent the time swimming laps while the kids were using the water slide. But I decided to attend one day. Yes, the kids spent a lot of time climbing and swooshing down the water slide but try as I could I saw very little of Ron swimming laps. The word was out among the young female lifeguards. Ron was always the heartthrob of all my brothers. I would kid him for hours about trying to find a girlfriend in every town he worked in. I am convinced he could do it. He was a 'chick magnet' especially in his swimming trunks.

Ron proved trustworthy in many ways both on and off the job. He was instrumental in helping secure an extra while at the Acid Plant. They needed some additional storage space at the plant. Ron interjected a brief comment about my crew having connections with a good mason in the area. The next thing I knew, we were constructing a new block storage structure next to the building we were already working on. A simple slab on grade block building with wood trusses and a shingled roof was on the fast track for completion/ But like every building I have worked on over the years, I was to learn something new while building it. I decided to perform the painting on the building since a good painter was not available on the time schedule I was committed to. The walls of the new building were sixteen feet tall. The need for a scissor lift or one-man reach lift was never more obvious. Riverton did not have much in the way of rental shops at that time. We resulted to extension ladders and long handle paint rollers. The cost savings I had anticipated began to dissipate quickly. The porous concrete block walls were soaking up our paint by the gallon. I had not sealed the block! By sealing the block, I could have cut the paint consumption in half. Live and learn! I can still see Willie working on top of that extension ladder up in the air fourteen feet without an air-less sprayer. It was a wonder we ever finished that job.

A TRUE FINISHER COMES ALONG

Once in a while I get a break when I can really use it. That happened when I bumped into Wade one day in downtown Riverton. He had been on the receiving end of hundreds of yards of concrete that I had batched. All the way from a Pulte housing project to the Riverton Wastewater Treatment Plant, we continued to cross paths. And here he was again, but this time he was looking for work. It didn't take long for me to snatch him up to help with my summer's projects. He had been finishing in the bay area of California since leaving his father's company. I had several small projects lined up and Wade would fit in nicely.

We started out relatively small in scope. We finished half a dozen driveways. I put Wade's experience to the test. He taught the crew how to use Wet Screeds and do away with inside pipe screeds that I had been using. By using a well-placed wooden grade stake and sweeping the fresh concrete instead of sawing it, we developed a great system. I would always control the pour by means of manning the chute. With one man in front of me and another behind, we could easily place the concrete within an inch of the final grade needed. Then Wade and I would sweep the excess along as our helpers raked the curl of mud just ahead of the screed board. There were no huge piles of concrete that needed shoveling or raking and the crew was not totally drained physically once the slab was to grade. This always proved advantageous by allowing more fresh manpower to the finishing steps. This also allowed us time in the afternoons to set up another pour for the following day. We were always trying to be as efficient as possible.

I began bidding curb and gutter work since Wade had extensive experience in setting forms and hand finishing the varying styles needed. Again we used a grade stake set every ten feet to maintain the critical flows needed in placing curb and gutter. I can remember a valley gutter job we did for the school district. They had hired it out several times over the past ten years and it was never done right. It consisted of five hundred feet of nearly flat grades with a valley gutter crossing the parking lot where the school bus routes formed each afternoon. The gutter never drained properly, it had numerous lakes that formed along its course and these would develop into solid sheets of ice in the winter season. I was approached with the problem.

I agreed to pour the valley gutter on a Saturday if they would remove the old concrete without disturbing the asphalt along either side. By doing it this way, I promised them that they would have the use of the parking lot by that Monday afternoon. I knew that their entire fleet of buses would drive over the fresh concrete with only 18 hours of cure time (normally it would take seven days minimum). I would have to get the batch plant to mix me up a brew of High Early Concrete to achieve the strength needed.

This would also place a burden on the placing crew to get the concrete down quickly before the hydration began. Once it started there was no looking back. It would set next to immediately and whatever shape it was screeded to that was the final shape. And since we only had a few inches of grade to work with, we had to be very precise in setting the flow line of the valley gutter. The wooden grade stakes were set using a tight string line with the intent of removing the stakes immediately following the screeding operation. The edging was eliminated so as to keep as much future runoff from getting under the valley gutter as possible.

The pour went like clock work. The trucks were right on schedule and the placing operations couldn't have been smoother. The Monday morning after the pour was spent saw cutting joints every ten feet across the valley to allow for future expansion and contraction. It looked beautiful when we were done. Now all we had to verify whether the school buses could cross the valley without hitting the frame of the bus on either side as they drove across. The speed would be monitored and policed very closely. The result was a great big Hoo-raw! We passed with flying colors. But I did notice in a few short weeks several speed bumps were installed to slow down the passenger cars and trucks as they were crossing the project. At too high a speed, the vehicles were bottoming out on one side or the other. But the concrete was holding up like a champion.

I continued to place curb and gutter, driveways, and building slabs through out the summer. Wade, Willie, Danny, and Brian made up my summer crew. We all got along really well and learned from every job we undertook. At the close of the summer season, I picked up a contract with the City of Riverton. We would be replacing a city block's worth of curb, gutter, and sidewalk. All the demo and soil prep was provided by the City so all we had to complete was the concrete work. The most unusual part of the whole thing was the street itself. The asphalt needed to stay in place so as not to impede the traffic in that part of town.

I took my concrete saw on to the jobsite first of all. I snapped a line the full length of the street and using a new asphalt blade in the saw, I cut the three inches of black asphalt as straight as an arrow. We then set the back form for the curb and gutter. Following the profile specified by the city we then poured the entire street length of curb and gutter in one day. The inspector was flabbergasted that we would even consider undertaking a 28 yard pour with only four men and then equally impressed that we turned out such a beautiful stretch of street. That left just the sidewalk.

After the sub grade was prepared and tested, we set our forms for another thirty-yard pour. The inspector was curious on how we would get the expansion joints installed during the continuous pour. After we explained our system to him, he agreed to give it at try. Again the four of us laid down the concrete including the felt expansion joints without a hitch. The sidewalk was five foot wide again with expansion joints every 100 feet. The control joints were tooled in every five feet as well leaving a satisfied inspector and a well-deserved weekend for the crew. But we must have been over confident, because we left about an hour too early.

We placed a couple of sawhorses at both ends of the sidewalk to prevent foot traffic from entering the sidewalk before it had gained enough strength. WRONG! A minute or two after we left for home, a knobby tired bicycle proceeded to jump the curb and then head right down the middle of the fresh concrete sidewalk. It was wet enough that a ½ inch groove was embedded into the surface. And if that wasn't bad enough he spun around and did the same thing in the opposite direction!

When I stopped by an hour later, I couldn't believe my eyes. My ego was shot with both barrels. I made a futile attempt to rescue the pour but it was too late. I made a trip or two around the neighborhood trying to determine who had been the culprit but to no avail! The only thing that could be done was to remove and replace the damaged sidewalk the following week. That simple mistake of leaving just an hour too soon had cost me close to ten thousand dollars! But it had to be replaced.

So reluctantly we began the removal and re-pour of the sidewalk. It was an expensive lesson. But guess what happened next. We were standing at the end of the street when a lone bicycler approached us but on the opposite side of the street. I didn't give him too much attention except when he turned and made a beeline straight towards the new sidewalk, which still hadn't cured yet. I happened to be holding a push broom that I was using to clean off the street. As the bicycle came speeding by me heading straight to the fresh concrete, I grabbed my broom handle and jabbed it straight into the front spokes of his bike. Needless to say he did not reach the sidewalk! He jumped up screaming bloody murder at me. I confronted him immediately and grabbed his bike along with the knobby tires that matched the damage that had been done the week before. I demanded to know where he lived. He refused to divulge anything. For whatever reason I chose to just let him go instead of involving the police. The damage had been done and hopefully by handling him in a caring manner we could prevent more damage to his future decisions.

But when school calls, the crew responded. Willie, Brian, and Danny all headed back to the books Wade and I prepared for the winter months. Just before I was going to lay off Wade, I landed a small remodel project. I don't normally do too many remodels but the size and the situation fit perfectly.

Bonnie was a friend from my associations on the city basketball league. She was working full time as well as her husband, leaving the kitchen and bathrooms available to us for the upgrade. Their home was immaculate and very clean from top to bottom. The kitchen and the bathrooms were somewhat dated but well maintained in every way. We felt somewhat inadequate to upgrade the kitchen and each bathroom to the twentieth century.

But that is where Bonnie diverged into the world of antiques. She wanted the style to reflect the farming culture she had been raised in and not the bright shiny new look of the turn of the century. She knew what she wanted but like so many housewives, couldn't explain it. But when she saw it, she knew whether or not it fit into her vision of her country abode.

We had to replace every door inside the home to a distressed, raised panel, wood door. They were quite expensive but that was what she wanted. Corian and granite countertops were just coming onto the market. But that was not what she wanted. She looked through hundreds of Formica chips and discovered a sample that was on the verge of being discontinued since it was not in the main stream of popular trends. We purchased the last sheets available from the Salt Lake City supply house. She wanted the backsplash and the front edge of the countertop to be an exposed hardwood stained to match the cabinetry.

The kitchen cabinetry needed to be re-used in order to enhance the charm of her country theme. But all the hardware needed to be replaced. She went from a modern looking hinge to a wrought iron surface mounted hinge and pull arrangement. The one thing that really threw me for a loop was the weathered impression that the older hinges left on the cabinetry. We tried numerous techniques to either conceal the old hinge location. By using one single door as a sample; we stained, then bleached, and then antiqued the finish trying to obtain the look she was after. We had converted a small outbuilding of Wade's into our cabinet shop. The final decision was not what I expected. She chose the finish that enhanced the weathered appearance of the old hinge location the most. I personally would have selected something else but she couldn't stop bragging about her 'Country Style' kitchen. She had a steady stream of friends and neighbors parading through the project to admire the as yet unfinished look.

The duration of the project was almost twice what I had estimated. But Bonnie insisted that the extra time be calculated into the monthly statements. And at the conclusion of the remodel, she was completely ecstatic about the end product. We even picked up some incidental work from Bonnie's friends that each had their own project to complete. But I am sure they did not have the funds available to match Bonnie's.

A quick incident that happened mid way through this remodeling experience. Wade is a smoker. I was somewhat intrigued by his choice of cigarettes. Wade always smoked Lucky Strikes the same brand that my Dad smoked until he died. I think they were the only two people that I knew that chose that brand from the hundreds that there were to select from. But he was hooked and I tolerated it just like I had when my Dad smoked during my younger growing up years.

And then completely out of the blue, Wade decides to switch brands. He wanted to switch from Luckys to hand rolling his own. I had pictured him choosing Camels or Marlboro but instead he chose Prince Albert in a can. And when I asked Wade why he was switching he replied," I can cut the cost of smoking in half by rolling my own" I replied that if he would just quit completely he could really save a ton. Wade just chose to ignore the obvious. He just kept on rolling his own smokes from that day on.

Shortly after our winter remodel, Wade informed me that he was taking his family and moving to Alaska! He claimed that he could make twice as much while working in Juneau than he was making in Wyoming. I was surprised because I had been paying him well above the rate for finishers in the lower forty-eight states. But he had already purchased their Winnebago and they were going to drive all the way to Alaska and see the sights. I tried to talk him out of it but his wife and kids really wanted to live in Alaska. So they loaded up in early June and headed north.(I would find out later that Wade's wife had a lover in Alaska and she skipped out as soon as they arrived there).

LOOKING FOR A PARTNER

I was becoming frustrated with the yearly ritual of locating a few good hands and then laying them off for the winter months. I needed to control the cash flow of my business and regulate a more even flow of incoming funds and out flowing expenses. I needed to grow as a company, which would allow me to use the talents I had acquired in school and over years of supervising building projects. So I began looking for more building projects that I could handle.

The very first project that I looked at required a bond. I opened up a dialogue with a local bonding agent. After lengthy discussions, it became obvious to me that in order to become a bonded contractor I had to prove that I financially did not need a bond. While at school in Provo, I learned that bonding companies are looking at three things in a contractor. They called them the three "C-s". The bonding agency looks for Character, Capacity, and Capital. I was told that I had plenty of the first two--- Character and Capacity. But my Capital was not liquid; it was all tied up in equipment, forms, and tools. Some how I had to have reserves available that could be used on a short-term notice.

I continued to look for larger projects to help bolster my cash flow needs. In the meantime I picked up a few home additions and residential upgrades. I finally was able to land a church remodel in Cowley that I could bond. I had too many small projects under contract in Fremont County to just walk away from so I hired a Superintendent to run the Cowley Remodel. Lane was looking for more local work but agreed to man this one out-of- town project for me.

Working on LDS churches is a completely different type of an experience. But since Lane was a good member of the church he stepped right in. Starting each day's work with a prayer is definitely unusual when compared to the rest of the world. The standards of cleanliness and personal hygiene are higher than expected. But we set down the rules and went right to work.

The doors that we had to replace were all wood but the frames needed to be replaced with hollow metal jambs. These jambs had to be grouted solid both for stability and fire resistance. We decided to try out a different technique than I had seen done before. Normally the jambs are set and then grouted in place. This can be both time-consuming and messy. We would skip a step and pre-grout the jambs before they were set. We only had eight to replace so the procedure shouldn't be that involved.

By using this improvised method, we were able to speed up the schedule by a week. Since we had to have the church accessible every weekend, the jambs were on our critical path. We had them set during our first week of construction. So far, so good.

The plumbing rough in was also on the critical path. That was one reason I hired Lane to run the remodel. He is a licensed plumber. Things were moving nicely. But things happen to the best laid plans of mice and men. The electrician that was under contract to wire the project, backed out at the last minute. I needed a licensed electrician and immediately. The only company that I could find was from Worland almost a hundred miles away.

The time delay for not having an electrician was really going to hurt unless something could be put in place and soon. Lane came up with the idea to 'one-side' the sheetrock ahead of the wiring. It was a step out of the normal way to sequence the job but it would allow work to continue while I put the electricians under contract.

Just as soon as the ink dried on the contract, I had a crew on-site roughing in the entire job. I was totally relieved when the local city inspector passed the rough-in inspection on the first pass. Now the rest of the sheetrock work could be completed. The job schedule was still tight but very feasible. The interior painting was completed and the drop ceilings were installed just ahead of the plumbing fixtures arriving.

Once the ceramic tile work was completed, the trimming out of the electrical and mechanical could begin. Again the shipping companies were delivering the finished products just like clockwork. It really felt good to have my ordering sequence match so closely with the field coordination that Lane was providing. The final completion deadline was met and I had my first bonded project under my belt.

But I was completely taken back when my bonding agent told me that my bid amount would not increase. I had proven that I could complete the contracts on time and under budget but they wanted to see a couple more jobs completed before the bonding ceiling would be raised. I left his office totally miffed. I spent the next week looking for a different bonding company but felt like I was starting all over again from scratch. I had to increase my liquid assets somehow.

About this same time I contracted with a local contractor to complete the concrete work for a new company that was opening up shop in the state. BTI was signed to haul trona to a Shoshoni terminal where the Burlington Northern Railways would transfer it into their railcars and haul it to the final destination. Apparently the Union Pacific Railroad had been hauling it from Sweetwater County to the same destination for years but their rates just kept climbing. BTI landed a huge contract to bypass Union Pacific, haul it in their semi-tractor trailers, and then use Burlington Northern to complete the route. Fremont County was in the trona business!

Fixter Construction was hired to design and remodel an office complex from the Gilpatricks who had closed their doors after fifty years in highway construction. The old office was to double in size and their shop and storage yard would be updated with state of the art maintenance equipment and a full over the road mechanics station. I would be working under Dave, who was the lead superintendent with Fixter.

I was using Willie again for the summer realizing that his services were temporary at best. I hired Kelly who showed considerable promise in concrete work. He had several years experience operating equipment, which I was in need of too. The concrete footings, walls, and slabs were completed without a hitch. Near the end of the concrete work, Dave approached me wanting to hire my crew to work by the hour in completion the project. I accepted it primarily because he promised to keep each of employed throughout the winter months.

So we became carpenters/laborers as the remodeling continued. We help remove the old brick on the existing building and assisting the masons to get their stonework underway. I was pleased that a few of my ideas were integrated into the project, which helped save monies and time. I wanted to stay involved in the construction of the atrium. The architect had developed the central atrium concept, which I had seen used throughout South America. The entire office arrangement was placed around the perimeter of the new addition. A two-story atrium was located at the center of the facility. Living flowers, shrubs, and trees were the center vocal point in the atrium, which took special implementation and maintenance.

This construction was unique because debarked tree trunks 24 inches in diameter were used as the main structure for the roof beams. I was intrigued at the structural attachment used to anchor the trees. An 18-inch long by one-inch hole was bored into the base of the trees. A fabricated steel anchor plate was embedded into the concrete columns which had a 7/8 inch steel rod attached vertically. The bored tree trunks were impelled on these dowels and the tops were secured using ½ inch thru-bolts that ran through the trees and the roof beams simultaneously. The atrium had skylights set at the roofline allowing plenty of natural light to enter the building. It was a one of a kind design and very well put together.

The only glitch happened when the two building were opened up as the combined office space. The existing building slab was an inch higher than the new floor! There was plenty of blame to go around but we needed a solution. The adjoining hallways were located near the front entrance. A portion of the new concrete floor was removed and a gradual ramp was placed in line with the new hallway. It went together as slick as a whistle. The change was practically un-noticeable to the public and their new office personnel. BTI has their local office located on the main highway-entering town with all their trucks passing in front, once going and once coming. It was well thought out if I do say so myself.

Following the completion of the BTI Facility, I continued to get calls for concrete work throughout the county. A foundation here, a driveway there, concrete needed everywhere. Kelly and I poured a split-level foundation and floor behind the Holiday Inn. I think it was the first time that I turned Kelly loose on finishing by himself. I was there the whole time working right beside him the whole way, but he was leading the pour so to speak. He decided how to approach the foundation, how far apart to schedule the mixer trucks, and placing the order based on his own quantity take-off. I needed to know how close he was paying attention at all the steps I went through on a given job.

We only had each other to rely on. I usually hired a few extra hands to help on a job that size. At the first troweling of the basement slab, we took a breather before we would normally hit it for the hard troweling. The owner just happened to stop by. He couldn't get over how perfect it looked and to imagine that we had been the only two men responsible. The job was a milestone in a relationship that I hoped would blossom again and again.

It wasn't long until I was forced to rely on Kelly and Willie on a different type of remodel. I had numerous bids out on a wide variety of projects ranging all across the county. I very seldom win 100 % of the jobs that I bid. I think that if I am awarded more than 75% of those bids that I am bidding too low and need to increase my margins. But this one particular bid came through on replacing vinyl siding. I had never installed this type of siding before and only bid it so as to remain in line for bigger projects from this particular individual. But when he wanted it completed before July, it really put a strain on my crews and concrete projections.

The local lumberyard had the materials ordered and since they would loan me the necessary specialty tools for its completion, I accepted it. Kelly and Willie both worked well together. They took on the siding project while Layne and I went to the far side of Lander to work on an oil field water purification structure. I expected the siding project to move slowly due to their inexperience with the system. I wasn't disappointed. But they were moving too slowly to reap any monetary benefits on the bid. I visited their job a few times in order to light the fire under them so to speak. It worked as the pace began to pick up.

The Water Purification System was between Lander and the Beaver Creek Oilfield. It required a 45-minute commute each day just to get to the jobsite. It was comprised of a series of concrete walls that ran parallel to each other and at different heights allowing the oilfield water to cascade across each weir while depositing the floating residue on the weirs before it returned to the holding pond. There were twenty such weirs spaced eight feet apart and ranging in heights from three to four feet high. But the tough part of the project was the length of the walls and the limitation of access to only one side of the structure.

The formwork and rebar placement was verily standard but the concrete placement presented a problem. Since the structure was over thirty feet wide, we could not pour the walls easily from the mixer's chutes as was typical. We needed a conveyor or pump to get the concrete to its proper place. We didn't have either one and the soonest I could obtain one was over two weeks out. I had to improvise. I brought all my employees to the pour and positioned them strategically along the walls to hand muck the concrete down the forms. I also added a super-plasticizer to the mix to help it flow as much as possible. It worked but each of our arms felt like limp noodles at the completion of the day. There IS more than one way to skin a cat! (So to speak)

The siding job was an eye opener. I learned to stay within my realm of knowledge and skills. I received numerous callbacks to come fix little incidentals on the home that shouldn't have been necessary. But Willie and Kelly were still talking to each other, which was good, and I was able to bid future work with this company manager.

A FIFTY-FIVE FOOT VIBRATING SCREED

Over the years I was always looking for a way to cut down labor costs and bid large slabs below my competition. I used my 25-foot steel screed whenever possible but it had its limitations. I had located a 55-foot aluminum screed that had some very definite advantages. It was lightweight, versatile, and since it was "used "the price was within my expectations. I took the plunge and purchased it!

The fact that it was modular really proved advantageous. It came with both ten and five foot modules that were completely interchangeable. I was using it on driveways as narrow as twenty feet and full slabs as wide as fifty feet wide. I would have never imagined a crew of five or six men could pour a slab that big in one day. But with a couple power trowelers it was now possible. My square foot concrete floor costs were the lowest in the county and the word spread. I was receiving calls left and right.

I can remember one slab in Dubois in particular. The slab was forty feet wide and one hundred feet long. The contractor that I was finishing for was responsible for the final grading and the purchase of the concrete itself. I had informed him to have the concrete ordered for six o'clock sharp on that Friday morning and we would be ready. We were a little late arriving there on Thursday but still knew we could set the forms and have the screed in place before night set in. He became nervous and called off the concrete delivery. We arrived and began setting forms in anticipation of a 6 A.M. pour time.

The superintendent drove by the job a little after 7 P.M. and was surprised to see us on-site working. He stopped to review what my plan was and then apologized profusely for having canceled the concrete order. After some frantic phone calls, he was able to secure a Noon delivery. I was upset to say the least primarily because the prime concrete finishing window had been lost. But Noon would have to work.

The following morning was spent lounging around the local Daylight Donut shop since the concrete wasn't coming until noon. The forms were in place and ready but the order had been changed without notice. I was somewhat familiar with the weather conditions around Dubois in the fall. And right on schedule, the wind began to blow at 10 A.M. And the wind can blow in Dubois. But we didn't have a choice now, the slab had to be placed since we were expected on a different job come Monday.

We poured out the fifty plus yards were laid as quickly as possible. The wind didn't die down at all but assisted in raising the silt and red sands of the site into a full-blown dust storm. But I had 4,000 square feet of concrete to finish, and had to do the best I could. The edges were tooled and worked by hand while my walk behind trowelers finished the interior of the slab. I am not sure that a pink slab was in the cards but that is what developed at the conclusion of the day. A beautiful rosy pink colored slab was the result due to the red blown conditions of the site. I am sure that if we had begun at 6 A.M., the wind would not have been a factor.

My aluminum screed continued to prove its usefulness. The next month I landed a bid for a thirty-foot wide circular driveway. It is really tough to get ten foot steel forms to bend into a circular configuration. So I set my steel straight forms as an outside screed and then used 6 inch wide Masonite siding to form the circular profile of the driveway. That combined with a dozen bundles of wooden stakes was just the ticket. A two hundred foot circular driveway that is the envy of the neighborhood!

Kelly continued to stand up to the rigors of concrete work and the hours that I demanded of my employees. I almost always saw the sun rising on one of my projects and 40 hours was a slow week for all my men. So I approached him one day with the proposal to join me as a full partner in the business. After much prayer and discussions back and forth, we threw in together. Skyline Construction was a partnership!

One of the first things we needed to do was acquire another pick-up. I fully planned on bidding twice the jobs that I was presently looking at. So off to Casper we went. We always made a stop to see what were new in hand tools. There always seemed to be a trowel, kneeboards, or edger that was just what we needed to make our jobs a step above the competition. We also looked at utility trailers but I still hadn't seen what I was looking for. It seemed like all the trailers available were less than eight feet wide. I wanted to stack my eight-foot concrete forms across the trailer to maximize the space.

In order to pull the 24-foot trailer I would need at least a ¾-ton pickup preferably with a fifth-wheel set up. We did find a used white F-250 that we thought was priced right. So before the day was finished, we were driving separate vehicles back to Riverton. I know that Ford trucks are notorious for needing repairs but we both agreed on the purchase.

PIONEER SQUARE IN WORLAND (BELL TOWER)

It was a good thing we had picked up that Ford because the very next week we landed a unique contract in Worland. Newel Sargent wanted to build a memorial to the town and the county by purchasing a city block at the main intersection of town. He envisioned a city park for public use completely landscaped and resident friendly. The first phase was a bell tower. Yes, a Bell Tower in the heart of Washakie County!

The design was for four separate towers extending twenty-plus feet into the air. The four towers needed to be well supported with massive structural concrete piers and footers. The same towers would then be tied together with structural steel cross members located ten feet off the concrete floor. The masonry work was the key to a successful project and a local mason won the bid. He came with an excellent reputation and the exact brick that Newel was looking for. It is amazing how things come together sometimes.

Kelly and I made numerous one hundred mile trips to Worland while working on the concrete and carpentry details of the project. It was a good thing that we had two contractor outfits that could be sent in different directions because that happened more times than I can remember. The mason on the Bell Tower was pushing the time envelope to the hilt. We still had some carpentry items to complete as well as the exterior sheetrock (Dens-Glas) to complete with just two weeks until the completion date arrived.

I can remember it very clearly because Kelly and I worked through one of those Wyoming blizzards to get the framing completed. Maybe you have been in one, where the snow isn't falling down in fluffy patterns, but whistling across the site behind thirty mile per hour Wyoming winds. But we were determined to get it completed, no matter how cold our hands and fingers became. I think it was half way between Thermopolis and Shoshoni before we could feel our toes and fingers responding to the heater in the truck as we drove back to Riverton.

Again we were blessed because the following week a warm Chinook wind engulfed the area allowing the sheetrock and painting to be completed on schedule. I can still hear the cadence of those electronic bells echoing for blocks around. Yes, I said electronic bells because the whole system was designed with a computer. Each tower had a Bell located high above the ground but they did not move at all. The system was computer guided and could be programmed to play just about any tune imaginable. It was completely state-of-the-art at the time. Stop by Worland on your next trip and see the masterpiece.

We finished this project just in time to head to Wapiti. Now where in the world is Wapiti, Wyoming? It is located about half way between Yellowstone National Park and Cody, Wyoming. We had landed a contract with the Forest Service to install six cattle guard crossings at various locations. And one of them was a Wapiti. I know it violated one of my parameters for staying within 100 miles of home but we still could get a few nights fishing if the weather held. And all the other structures were in Fremont County.

The scope of the contract was to pour the concrete box for the cattle guard to rest upon, purchase and install the specification unit, and backfill the entire box to compacted specifications. If everything went well the whole project could be completed in less than a week. That left a day to fish, and a day to check out the local utility trailer inventory. It was suppose to have what I had been looking for in width and durability. (We did swing through Cody on our way home and purchased a brand new trailer.)

There must have been a hiccup associated with this job but I can't remember it for the life of me. We stayed at a moderately priced cabin near Wapiti that allowed us to cook our own meals otherwise it was a thirty mile commute for dinner. The area was just like I remember it with the North Fork River running clear and cold. The fish always seem to be hungry and the peaks all had received a good covering of snow. It was a good way to end the summer.

STEEL BUILDINGS (WEDGCOR)

That winter was spent getting trained on a new metal building franchise that we wanted to bring into the Wind River Basin. Wedgcor offered us a generous package and we committed to making it work. Part of the package deal included a tour of their factory and a week's training on the erection and handling of their buildings.

Kelly and I took a couple of days to drive to North Dakota for their plant tour. I was impressed with the latest techniques they were using to fabricate the columns, beams, and girders we would be using in the erection of their buildings. It was all high quality and coordinated. I couldn't wait to get our first building. Just a quick note about North Dakota. It is as flat as any country I have ever seen. The locals there claim their state tree is the 'power poles' that stretch along the highways. I can now relate because that is the only thing I saw that even closely looked like a living tree.

The erection and sales training was to be held in Denver during the following month. We were treated like royalty while there. A very nice motel with excellent meals and comfortable rooms was all provided. But the package only included two meals, breakfast and lunch. We were on our own for supper. No problem, the motel was located right in the middle of nearly a dozen different restaurants! We had a hard time choosing which cuisine to sample. It was Italian, Chinese, Barbecued Ribs; all you can eat buffets, and a steak house to die for. We must have gained five pounds in that week alone. The training was very detailed and they invited us back again next year, only we had to pay for the extra training and hospitality.

Wedgcor had a very enticing incentive package for new franchise holders. If we could sell over certain dollar amount then a very substantial discount was available. We left Denver certain we could sell well above the minimal amount needed for the discount. But upon bidding a half dozen jobs around Fremont County, we realized that their building prices weren't as competitive as we had been led on to believe. But we did sell a small building right off the bat to an outfitter from Dubois.

We had about a month to get ready for the building package to arrive. The concrete work was a piece of cake since we had done dozens of slabs of comparable size all over the county. But the forklift we had reserved from the local rental agency was rented out from under us. We scrambled to locate a forklift to erect the building with upon arrival. We did find one in Riverton and using our heavy-duty trailer and Ford truck were able to transport it to Dubois on time. The erection went well but upon completion and totaling up the costs we discovered that we had only broke even. No big profits on this job! We needed to get more efficient with our skills or this investment was going to cost us money instead of making up for the cash flow difficulties of the past.

Our sales efforts were very concentrated over the next few weeks. But the competition was just as aggressive. The only sales we were able to secure was to Kelly's father, Dennis, and he wanted that erected in Southern Utah of all places. But we had sold enough to obtain the discount offered by our building supplier, Wedgcor. We would put the Southern Utah issue on hold until winter.

We were also able to secure some miscellaneous projects that needed steel siding and other that used steel roofing. Our learning curve was very steep. We picked up some specialized electric tools as well. A nibbler to cut circles and specialty holes in the steel panels and also an electric sheer to cut the panels off on a straight line. It was preferred to order the panels from the factory 'pre-cut' to the desired length but that wasn't always possible.

We put these tools to work on a somewhat different steel siding project at the local Smith's grocery store. We were hired to replace the front soffit of the building, not the roof or some of the siding but the bottom soffit right at the high traffic location of the 24-hour Smith's.

That project had a couple of nuances that were a challenge. The columns at the entrance were hand cut around which was expected. The biggest challenge was with the fire suppression system. There were a dozen live sprinkler heads located in that soffit that heeded to remain active. We had to cut them into the metal panels with complete accuracy. One mistake and a hundred dollar metal panel was destroyed. What made it difficult was the corrugations in the metal panels. Several of those sprinkler heads landed directly on the corrugation high point making it very difficult to get an accurate circle hole cut to fit.

But probably the toughest part of the whole job was working at a store that had a bakery. The store vents the bakery fumes out the front of their store on purpose. The aromas of freshly cinnamon rolls and loaves of specialty breads made it extremely costly to work there. We must have tried every product they prepared at the bakery. I was afraid to account for the weight gain we both realized while working at Smith's Bakery.

PIONEER SQUARE (SITE IMPROVEMENTS)

We continued to market our metal buildings but it was a definite uphill battle. But we did manage to secure the second half of the Worland Pioneer Square Project. It consisted of site improvements to the entire city block and a restroom facility for public use. Since the Bell Tower was already in place, we would need to protect that masterpiece; then pour exposed-aggregate sidewalks, erect a retaining wall, completely landscape the site, and erect several architectural features. Even before we had begun the project, Newel Sargent had set a date for the grand opening ceremony that had entire state coming. The pressure was on the complete the work on time!

The restroom facility was simple and efficient. A block building with a metal roof was the basic premise. But the architect wanted to place his stamp on the building. There were more than four corners to the final plan. A raised panel roof system with a Dutch Hip profile. The interior was clean and very modern looking. Stainless Steel plumbing fixtures along with toilet partitions were specified. A vandal resistant bathroom accessory package completed the twentieth century look of the public restrooms.

There was a lengthy meandering sidewalk that fit in perfectly to the desires of Newel Sargent. I had purchased a fifty-five gallon drum of surface retardant to apply to top of the special concrete mix. It was a very rocky mix design with additional 'seed rock' that was placed directly ahead of the screed board. This was then bull floated flat and the retardant sprayed over the entire surface. The entire sidewalk was allowed to hydrate and cure for the next 12 hours where upon the top surface was washed clean leaving the aggregates exposed for the public to enjoy.

There was a Pioneer Square Committee that was interested in setting up a trust fund to guarantee funding for the maintenance and beautification of the Pioneer Square far into the future. They accomplished this by selling brick pavers to businesses, individuals, and supporters of this city project. These pavers were then placed in two foot by three foot recessed boxes along the extent of the meandering sidewalk. It was quite ambitious if I do say so myself. It was quite remarkable to walk along and read the names of donors that had their names cast into the brick pavers. I noticed that many were even from out of state.

But the most remarkable feature that I enjoyed above all others was a life size metal statue of a Horse-Drawn Fresno. A Horse-Drawn Fresno was used by the early settlers to cut irrigation canals and ditches from the river to water the crops that were planted throughout the area. An artist had been hired in Montana to fabricate the entire work of art from steel panels. It was welded and soldered together using only steel components. The idea being was to allow the steel to rust thus giving it a more historical patina. I personally enjoyed the life-size dog that was positioned just behind the farmer and his horse. The dog is turning to chase a statue of a jackrabbit that can be seen leaving the scene. This was all done very professionally and again completely life-sized with the detail exquisite.

Additional statues and interpretive gazebos were stationed around the square depicting the history of the valley. The last time I visited the Pioneer Square; I noticed how huge all of the trees were that had been planted throughout the project. I also noticed some additional statues that had been added since the completion. A full sized statue of a pioneer woman was very appropriate since so much of their sacrifices and work have gone un-noticed over the years. Newel Sargent has definitely given Worland something to be proud of.

I also made two other stops along that route. I couldn't help myself. About a mile from where I used to live, I received this uncontrollable urge to pull over at the Skyline Memorial Turn-around. It never failed but each morning as we left Riverton, I would be reviewing the agenda for the day in my mind. At this exact spot on the highway, I would remember a tool or some materials or something else needed for the day's work. We turned around dozens of times at that very turn out on the highway to return and load up the item or items that we had forgotten.

Another landmark along the way to Thermopolis/Worland was the Fast Lane Convenience store in Shoshoni. I am convinced that my crew single handedly kept them in the black financially. We would stop twice a day, one coming and one going. The store always made sure to have a good supply of Honey Buns and Ding Dongs for the hungry workers who couldn't resist. Chocolate and strawberry milk was high on the list of the ten most commonly purchased snacks while in Shoshoni. I fully expected some of my oil field worker friends to walk out of that door just as we were driving up to the curb.

COMMERCIAL REMODELING

The upcoming winter months posed an added burden now. The company had two families to support during the lean construction months. A few incidental remodels were secured but it was not enough. I began looking at just about anything to bring in some much needed revenues. Fixter Construction always seemed to have adequate work for their employees and even a little extra. The local Key Bank wanted to remodel their main floor and I guess I was in the right place at the right time. I did not bank there as a contractor or as an individual but John Fixter did. He approached me as a sub-contractor who was not afraid to work after hours. And he was right. The entire remodel had to be done between 7 P.M. and Midnight. It looked like a three-month job at least. A large part of the project comprised in electrical and heating upgrades. But the main floor of the bank needed to be redone. A guy could get seasick just rolling across that floor too fast.

After looking at the situation, I recommended a leveling topping coat be applied in lieu of a demolition and re-pour. The bank manager was completely on board to such a suggestion not wanting to close the bank for any period of time. But several eyebrows were raised when I suggested it, each belonging to non-believers. I had laid floor stone on a floor back in Cody and I knew what the product was capable of.

The main floor and the lobby were divided up into quarters for the leveling operation. Since no grinding was permitted, the high spot of each quarter was identified using my transit. And then the floor stone compound was hand mixed five gallons at a time. A straight creed rod was used and the compound was spread out using the high point of the floor as the screeding point. A pink colored boding agent was added to the mix which made it very easy to see and since the floor was going to be re-carpeted anyway it didn't make any difference that the floor had a pink hue to it for a few days. Personally I think the gals that worked at the bank were proud of their new Pink floor.

The entire topping coat took four different nights to complete. The durability of the floor depended on the quality of the finishers. It had to be hand troweled and the more passes over the floor the better. The topcoat was a little different than hydrating concrete since it responded to water being troweling into the final pass. The surface was tight and very durable ready for the weekend carpet layers. And of course I had to be there in case there were any unforeseen problems. The only problem we encountered was with the pizza that was delivered. THERE WAS NOT NERE ENOUGH!

The next few weeks went off without a hitch. The cabinetry arrived on schedule and the project was a huge success. But like usual all the profits went to the General Contractor and I was not that man. I had planted a seed with Fixter that would bear fruit down the road.

We didn't have to wait long. Fixter hired us to frame a custom home for him on the Riverton Golf Course. It was in a high profile neighborhood and atypical. It was a two-story home with a gazebo roof style on one of the wings. We were excited about the chance to show off our carpentry skills. Right at the get go, we were put to the test. We had just completed the main floor sheathing when it started to rain. No big deal, we would wait out the storm and return to framing the walls. But the rain didn't stop for the better part of ten days. The owner was concerned about the integrity of the floor sheathing with that much water exposure.

The local engineering firm was called out to access the damage. After their inspection, they pronounced the OSB sound but warned of any future moisture exposure. The finish flooring products might not adhere to the high moisture content of the subfloor. I recommended two things that I thought would help the issue. Paint the subfloor with a cheap enamel paint and then over lay the subfloor with a thin plywood veneer. Both recommendations were approved.

The gazebo roof was going to present some interesting challenges. It was on the second story and they wanted it to have engineered trusses to satisfy the local building officials. Again I made a simple suggestion to accomplish the goal. Instead of trusses designed on a 24-inch layout. Engineer a truss at each of the eight ridge points and then using Simpson hangers place 2 x 8's across the span on 16-inch centers. The truss designer liked the idea and the general contractor was able to pocket a few extra dollars in the process. That proved to be a win-win situation for everybody involved.

We were able to complete the project on time and under budget! I also learned an important safety lesson. A steel shanked hammer is ideal for doing concrete formwork but the vibrations caused by repetitive blows can damage the human elbow. I switched to a wooden-handled framing hammer and the physical problem disappeared almost immediately. I became a believer!

WYOMING PIONEER HOME REMODEL

I had focused for months on buildings and work to carry me through the cold winter months. My bonding company continued to work with me, but I was on a short leash so to speak. I needed more bonding capacity and all seemed to be centered on my liquid assets. They were improving with each project that I completed. Of the many bids that I had out, I was successful in securing a remodel in Thermopolis. It was for the State of Wyoming and involved a fire upgrade to the Wyoming Pioneer Home.

The facility is located on 5 1/2 acres in the Hot Springs State Park and very close to the two mineral spring swimming pools that are an attraction for the entire area. They have over one hundred beds available with most being used at all times. The ratio of Female to male residents is at 2:1. And each of the residents is accepted following an application process that looks very closely at a limited income basis. There are considerable regulations and rules that have to be in place to keep the facility open.

The facility is very well equipped and well staffed. They have large rooms designed to receive a patron's own furniture and accessories. It has a large kitchen/dining room wing, a beauty parlor, barbershop, recreational facilities and a well-stocked library wing. The security was very well maintained and as we would find out, the fire alarm system is tied directly into the Hot Springs Fire Department. It is all situated on a huge landscaped section of the State Park there in Thermopolis.

The scope of the remodel was to upgrade the building to the State Fire Code at the time. That included replacing dozens of doors with fire-rated units. Also several walls had to be placed in their hallways to meet the latest fire requirements. The hallway and entry flooring needed to be replaced due to wear and tear, and some exterior improvements were needed for the accessibility of the patrons to all of the amenities of the Pioneer Home.

Prior to being able to begin work, all of the workers needed to be vetted and security checks conducted. It seems like the paperwork on most government jobs is twice what the private sector needs. But that is just the way it is, as long as everybody has the same standards to comply with. I was never worried about any of my employees since I had run checks on each of them before. I had a pretty good idea of what red flags would come up by hiring from shady sources. I was prepared to complete the contract with Willie, Kelly, Wayde, and myself as the only labor force needed.

The necessary orders were placed with companies I had worked with in Casper. The fire-rated doors and jambs was the largest ticket item for the job. I had to order the hardware separate because the division of work was completely different. The hardware also had a specific detail associated with each item. They each had to match the style and model of the existing hinges, locksets, and openers. It just so happened to be Schlage, which again was the most expensive. By the time all the panic bars, push plates, and grab bars were ordered it was going to cost a pretty penny.

While we were waiting for the specialty items to arrive, we began framing in the new partitions across the existing hallways. The sure thing about being a small contractor is needing to perform a wide variety of tasks. The job was too small to need separate subcontractors for the framing, sound insulation, sheet rocking, taping, and painting. That would prove beneficial in acquiring many of the smaller projects around the area. But the electrical work had to be performed by a licensed electrician. I hired Wesco, the same electrician I had used in Worland. He was available and I felt he would be fair in his pricing.

So step-by-step, we moved through the remodeling of the Wyoming Pioneer Home. Come to find out, the project had bid three times previously but was always over budget. This fact allowed us to post the lower bond to bid the project but would pose additional challenges, as we would find out.

The whole reason for the upgrade in the first place was to comply with the current State Fire Code. The majority of the doors needed to be replaced with one-hour Fire-rated doors. But for some reason the Fire Marshall had not insisted on replacing the hollow metal jambs with fire-rated hollow metal units. This was my first real brain scratchers on the project.

For some reason, which is not clear to me even to this day, most of the hinges in the existing jambs had been welded in place! So I had to cut out the welded hinges and weld new hinges back in their place. That was just plain wrong but I didn't have a choice since they wouldn't pay for new knockdown frames. I even made a demonstration for the in-house director and the fire marshal showing the speed and efficiency of the available knockdown jambs. But try as we may, we were unsuccessful in getting that change order approved. So we were placed in a corner of welding inside an occupied structure. Safety was of paramount concern.

The safety of the residents was delicate at best. But we had several problems to solve. Welding generates huge amounts of heat. And we would be welding adjacent to combustible materials. Welding also generates varying amounts of smoke that are harmful when inhaled. And most portable welding machines need 220-volt power to run them properly. We only had 110-volt outlets with an occasional panel located too far distant to be practical for the use of the conductors needed. So I turned to Star-Tech a company that I had completed various contracts for in the past. He not only had the solution but a certified welder to perform the specialized welding needed.

CONSTRUCTION HICCUPS

I needed to acquire a Hepa Vacuum cleaner that could handle the smoke and fumes. By putting a man with Wayde (the certified welder) equipped with the vacuum cleaner and a fully charged fire extinguisher the pathway was opened to complete the entire interior welding. So Kelly and Wayde were teamed up to perform the welding task. It was just beginning to look like a well-designed plan when another hiccup occurred. Kelly and Wayde were both younger than Willie or I. Apparently some of the friskier female residents decided they needed to take advantage of the situation. Every time I went to inspect their progress on the welding, I would find them inside the ladies apartments eating cookies or pie and listening to Zamfir, a laid back pan flute performer that really turned on the elderly single ladies. I almost burst out laughing at the sight of my young employees being wooed by the elderly gals on that floor. I guess I was somewhat to blame because I had given my crew the admonition to 'bend over backwards to make the residents comfortable' during our presence there. But I had to get the director involved since it was breaking one of the home's regulations. No male visitors inside the apartments un- attended! We all laughed our selves silly as we drove home that night. Kelly and Wayde had new girlfriends in Thermop!!! (Don't tell their wives!)

The work was progressing and the doors in the "D" Wing were all hung in spite of the female distractions. We began work in the basement area next. There were not that many doors to hang or that many jambs to replace but we would end up spending as much if not more time in this wing than in the previous sector. This section of the Pioneer Home contained the library and the laundry facilities. The patrons used the library exclusively, while the laundry was completely off limits to any resident.

The laundry had a staff working full time and even then they had a hard time keeping up with the demand of all 108 rooms. And then we showed up to replace their only door to the hallway with a new double set of hollow metal doors. The hardest thing to accept was the need for after-hours security. The machines were not coin operated and all the supplies were kept in a locked storage room across the hallway. But the existing door had been wired for security and fire alarms, so we had to maintain this profile for the new doors.

We began the demolition with as much care as can be given this type of work. The local fire department insisted that the system remain Live during the entire project. We were to become personally acquainted with the Fire Chief and Fire Captain but for all of the wrong reasons. The Fire System was a Silent System. It did not sound any alarms at the Pioneer Home but instead would trigger a panel down at the station and they would respond immediately.

During our demolition of the laundry door and jamb, we nicked the signal wire. Out of nowhere a half dozen fully clothed firemen burst on to the scene. Of course there was no fire and the zone where the alarm had sounded was deactivated then reset after the signal wire was repaired. That simple operation took the better part of two hours. The whole Pioneer Home was on lockdown for the two-hour ordeal. We received a black eye over the whole thing and it was totally unnecessary. But the following week, when we were installing the new hollow metal jamb, we nicked the wire again. The same two-hour emergency started the residents into a state of fretful worry. But still the system remained active. No fire watches or zone deactivations were approved. Talk about frustrating! After much grief that laundry room was complete.

I guess looking back on the whole thing; we deserved more stringent coordination with the maintenance staff. But what we received was a complete staff hawking. By hawking I mean we were being watched from every angle imaginable. And our most persistent nemesis was the librarian. We had work to do along her wing, but she was forever delivering books down each and every hallway. It seemed like wherever we were working she was peeking around corners and finding fault with every little error she could find. We finally complained to the director about her vendetta against us. She agreed to spend more time in the library and not being such a nuisance. Willie in his pleasant way had given her a nickname. Once the nickname of 'Conan the Librarian' was pronounced by Willie, the die was cast. She will be remembered as "Conan" for the rest of eternity.

CONSTRUCTION HICCUPS

There were a few doors at the Pioneer Home that were not scheduled to be replaced but just to receive a matching lockset. A very simple task that could be done by an average carpenter in a small amount of time. But my good friend Murphy decided that he needed to get involved. You remember Murphy the one that gets anything that can go haywire, to do just that. A few non-residential rooms were scheduled to get those new locksets. One of those was to the beauty parlor.

On that particular day, I was installing a whole wing of locksets only. The barbershop, some linen closets, a broom closet, and their beauty parlor. It was equipped to handle three ladies at a time. Try as I might I couldn't secure a time that day where the room was not in use. So I explained to the beautician that it would only take ten minutes to remove the old lockset and then install the brand new set. So I gathered up the necessary hardware and tools, for a quick in and out appearance at the beauty parlor.

I had installed a dozen or so of this particular lockset and knew the procedure or at least I thought I knew it. I must have been in a hurry to get that one done because right at the critical installation moment when the tumbler and the spindle are engaged, I felt a snap inside the lockset itself. I must have let out a gasp or an" Oh, No" because the entire room became deathly quiet. I then hear all four of the ladies in the room begin to exclaim,

"What was that you said?"
"Is there something wrong with the door?"
"Are we locked inside for good?"
"How are we going to get out of hear?"
"Are we going to miss dinner? They are fixing my favorite today."
"Do you think anybody will rescue us?"

I stood up and began to reassure them that I would do what was necessary to get us all out of the beauty parlor as quick as possible. And then I returned to the problem. I can remember thinking to myself. I can't believe that I am locked inside the beauty parlor with four seventy-year-old ladies and can't find a way out! After what seemed like an eternity, I finally was able to separate the spindle from the tumblers and punch the tumblers free from the door itself. Then with access to the spindle, I was able to slide it back and swing the door open. I can still hear the ladies clapping as the door opened. How embarrassing! As the ladies were buzzing about their adventure, I replaced the missing part and quickly installed the lockset for good. And then I made myself scarce while the Pioneer Home settled back down to their normal quiet routine.

Another of the critical items that the Fire Marshall wanted installed was a series of double doors that would isolate the wings of the building during a fire. These double doors had to have at least a 1-½ hour rating to satisfy code. They were also designed to remain open during working hours and rigged to close automatically during a fire. This was accomplished with a magnetic hold-open on each door and a door closer attached to the top of each door. The hardware package for each door would require a small wagon to carry it all. It had locks, panic bars, and push plates, automatic closers, smoke seals, sweeps, and hold opens for each and every location.

The final completed package was a thing of beauty but one wrong measurement and the whole door was ruined. So remember measure twice and cut once!

There were six sets of these corridor packages that we had to install. It was time consuming but we were finally finished. That is except for the testing of the fire system in its entirety. The PA System was used to inform everyone that a test of the new Fire System was going to follow and to please stand clear of all the doorways. Then after a few seconds the Test button was punched. The horns blasted, the strobes flashed and all the automatic fire doors slammed shut. The system passed on the first try! We were successful! Both the Director and the Fire Marshal were satisfied with the end result. The Wyoming Pioneer Home was again operating according to latest Fire code!

FT. WASHAKIE MEDICAL CLINIC

At the conclusion of the remodel in Thermopolis, I planned a family vacation to see my Mom in Provo, Utah. It had been a while since we had seen her and all the family was looking forward to the break. Of course my children wanted to see Grandma Bear again but a little incentive was also included in the visit. Provo has a huge water park called Seven Peaks, which would fit right in as a summer vacation. So off we went to brave the Utah freeways and see if the slides at Seven Peaks were as tall and exciting as everybody claimed they were.

We arrived without incident in Provo. We couldn't help but remember a similar excursion years earlier that had all my children eager to see Salt Lake City. As we dropped down Parley's Canyon into the heart of the Salt Lake valley, Tia looked out across the scene of endless subdivisions, highways, and urban smog and exclaimed," What a mess!" Everybody had a good laugh then and each time we drive through Salt Lake we can't help but reminisce and get another chuckle at the observation of our young daughter.

Mom as is her trademark had a picnic all ready for us in her backyard. We sat in the cool of her fruit trees eating and talking about the good ole' days in Cody. My children could hardly keep their excitement bottled up. The Call of the Peaks was ringing louder and louder the more we waited. So the scheduled water invasion was set for the following day at 10 o'clock sharp.

We live in Riverton and water slides are not very common to Wyoming. We have a few close enough to visit once in a while but the have Seven major slides in one location was indeed special for each of my children. We were totally enjoying the variety of the water facilities when over the P A System an announcements was blared over the entire park, "Would Dan Barrus please come to the office as soon as possible!"

My first reaction was," Who knows that I am even here at the Seven Peaks Resort? " Then my kids all wanted to know what I had done wrong. I think they equated it to being called to the Principal's office in school. So I left the family to their fun and walked nervously to their administration offices.

Upon arriving at the front office, I was handed a short note and a phone number. To call collect as soon as possible. The number was not from Riverton but somewhere in Montana since it had a Montana area code listed. Cell phones were not yet a common commodity so I used the office telephone to make the long distance call to Billings, Montana.

The owner of Stallings Construction greeted me. He proceeded to explain the purpose of the phone call. Stan was an Indian-owned construction company that had been awarded a government contract to remodel a BIA Medical Facility in Ft. Washakie. The project was set to begin immediately but his local superintendent had been caught stealing antlers off the reservation. He was ordered to replace his super or lose the contract. My name had surfaced as a possible replacement. And then without a minute to catch my breath he asked, " How soon can you start?"

I was caught totally off-guard. But after stammering for a minute or two, I agreed to meet him in Ft. Washakie on the next Tuesday at noon. When I returned to relay the jest of my experience, all the kids could say was, "Augh! And cut our vacation short?" I explained the importance of the message and committed to make it up to them as soon as possible.

So the following day we returned to Riverton and the preparations for my interview in Fort Washakie. The town is located at the base of the Wind River Mountains and completely surrounded by the Wind River Indian Reservation. The Western side of the reservation is the home of the Eastern Shoshone Indian tribe while the Arapaho Nation lives on the Eastern half. The town itself had grown from a meager beginning as a military fort used during the Indian Wars of the 1800's.

The town of Ft. Washakie is not that large with only a few hundred inhabitants. Most of the members of the tribe live on scattered sites spread out along the farmland and sagebrush flats that constitute the reservation. We agreed to meet at the BIA Headquarters to conduct the negotiations. I use the term negotiations very loosely. I had a few items in mind before we started but his initial offer was far and above anything I could have imagined. The only real item not addressed with his offer was transportation. I wanted to use my own transportation so as to be free to divert for personal business if the need would arise. Stan again surprised me by including a company credit card to cover fuel and repair costs along with an allowance that would more than cover my use of the truck I was driving.

Stan and I promptly proceeded following the signing of the agreement over to the office of Jim Sorensen, BIA Supervisor. Jim had been stationed in Ft. Washakie for a dozen years or more and knew just about everybody and everything needed to keep the project moving. We walked to the site where a licensed surveyor was engaged in staking out the project. He knew what he wanted and had taken charge following the release of the offending superintendent.

Stan had a laser level ready to leave with me so the excavation could proceed without interruption. Shoshone Enterprise was scheduled to begin breaking ground in the morning. All I had to do was show up. So with a laser level, a set of the plans, and a copy of the TERO regulations; I was in place to begin a new direction as a contractor in Fremont County.

Those first few days were spent in shooting grades for the Indian operators and studying the approved plans. I was pleased to see every promise mad to me being promptly fulfilled. Stan seemed to really know what he was doing. The excavation was quite simple for this project. It was a site located on an old riverbed and consisted in very little overburden to remove and then several feet of clean gravels to be removed from the town site. I also took the opportunity to test the local TERO agent at her abilities.

I called in and requested a couple of journeyman form setters be ready to begin on that upcoming Monday. I was put on notice when I had to explain what a form carpenter would be required to do when he arrived. I also requested a good laborer to assist the carpenters and myself during the excavation work. Up and until that point I had been quite pleased at the knowledge and abilities of the heavy equipment operators that were on my project.

But that Monday morning was a disaster waiting to happen. The three Indians that arrived were all three late and the supposed carpenters did not own a single tool to their name. I put the laborer to work cleaning up trash and debris from all over the site, while I called to complain about the lack of tools/experience of the two men she had sent to me. She agreed to have them return the next morning with tools and safety equipment to prove they were capable carpenters.

They all three returned the following morning with brand new hard hats and shiny new carpenter's aprons with their own hammers. I put them to work building a landing complete with a two-story flight of stairs. They really didn't have a clue where to begin or how to proceed. So I proceeded in showing them step-by-step instructions what they needed to do.

The two laborers that remained spent their time grading and leveling the footing excavations. Since the excavators had used a bucket with new teeth installed, the bottom of the trenches had been disturbed. The first three inches of native gravels needed to be re-compacted. Moisture was applied via a garden hose and a jumping jack compactor consolidated the loose materials.

But Jim Sorensen wasn't satisfied with the result. He wanted more compaction and more water applied to the footer trenches. He made arrangements to flood the entire footing areas with six inches of standing water. A fire hydrant was located some fifty yards away. The local firehouse had extra fire hose, which was attached to the hydrant, and the entire excavation was flooded. I allowed the procedure because in years past this same type of sub-grade had proven pervious to water allowing the extra gallonage to pass straight through without affecting the density of the native gravels.

The testing agency from Riverton wanted a means to verify compaction since their gauges didn't provide the comfort level that Jim Sorensen wanted. Shoshone Enterprises sent a front-end loader to the job site once the water had completely penetrated the sub-grade. The three yard front bucket of the loader was filled with soils and began a systematic proof rolling of the excavation. The Inberg-Miller Engineer visually observed the entire procedure and documented everything. Jim Sorensen was completely satisfied. By working with the on-site engineers and the governing agency, a trust was developed that would serve us well throughout the entire project.

The very next day additional carpenters were sent to the site from the TERO office to begin the setting of footing forms. It became evident from the get go that a foreman was needed that had some hands-on experience. And so far I did not have anybody even close to that caliber on the crew. I was trying to do my scheduling work and lead the forming crew at the same time. I could not see any progress.

That next Monday following payday was a typical occurrence on the reservation. Of the eight carpenters hired only five returned to work. So I notified the TERO office one more time and voiced my frustration. The next day brought a ray of hope however. Ronny showed up to work. He had his own tool bags and they resembled tools that had been used for years. It took him less than an hour to organize the manpower, set up the laser by himself, and actually begin reading the structural drawings. I had my foreman at last!

Once the forms began taking shape, I hired Ronny's brother to begin sorting the rebar deliveries and busting the rods into place. Things were looking up. The footers were poured and we were ready to erect wall forms. The foundation plan called for nine-foot tall walls. I discussed the issue with my Billings office and received the approval to construct ten-foot forms on site. The Oldman brothers both had experience in the snap tie system.

The formwork was progressing nicely when the TERO officer in charge decided to pay us a visit. She had only been on the job for five minutes when she called me over to change some things. She informed me that the TERO regulations that we were working under required equal numbers of Shoshone Tribal members as Arapaho. I had thirteen men working with eight of them being Arapaho. I needed to hire three more Shoshone members immediately! I had read the TERO regulations entirely and had not seen that regulation contained in the document. I asked her to show me where that 50/50 regulation was written. She could not!

She promptly issued me a citation for violating their tribal laws and left to bring in the tribal police to shut the job down. I sent all the workers home for the day and placed an urgent phone call to Stan in the Billings office. I explained the situation in detail to Stan. He responded in total support of my actions and concluded the call with, " I will be there in the morning to handle the problem!"

Billings is a good six-hour drive from Ft. Washakie. But bright and early the next morning, Stan drove onto the job loaded with two-dozen roses and two pounds of Russell Stover Chocolates! I asked him if I needed to fire any of the employees or maybe just hire another three Shoshone members. He simply answered, " Just go about your work and I will handle the TERO people."

Right after lunch, Stan returned to the site with the TERO officer and a couple of Business Council Members in tow. They spent close to an hour walking the site and discussing the issues. I noticed them all shake hands and leave the same way they had arrived. I was called over for a quick chat with Stan. He informed me that a mutual agreement exists between the two Indian Business Councils that equal numbers of both tribes need to be working on the project. But for the time being the unspoken agreement would be overlooked. But the next hires on the project needed to be Shoshone members. He also informed me that I really needed to hire a couple of the relatives from the same family as the TERO officer. (Politics even exist on the Wind River Indian Reservation) The hiring issue practically took care of itself on every payday. Those that really wanted to work would return to work and those only wanting some quick cash did not!

By the time the floor system was in place, I had a evenly numbered crew that really worked well together. And just in time too. That next week we received 18 inches of a wet snow overnight. That was unusual for September! I spent the early morning hours buying up all the snow shovels I could find. The next day was spent shoveling and clearing snow off the newly completed wood floor. The

Indian help proved a real blessing. The framing was again ready to proceed. The walls were all laid out with the top and bottom plates cut and ready for studs when we got hit with another twelve inches of snow and winds to go with it. The entire week was spent digging out of the freak storm. If this was going to continue, it would prove to be a long winter.

I was in contact with the head office in Billings and they were concerned about getting enclosed before the winter months descended upon us. They informed me that two of their top framing carpenters would be arriving in the morning to help out. They stepped in and took charge of the framing details. Hail guns, wall jacks, and every power tool needed to fast track that building arrived with them. The walls shot up over night. They knew the delivery date of the truss package from Montana and were going to be ready.

I was watching the weather forecast very closely. I wasn't sure we could get dried in before Thanksgiving. My experience in Wyoming dictated that a storm would arrive sometime during that last week of November. I was glad that it decided to wait until after the turkey was gone because we completed the exterior framing on the Wednesday before. We could now concentrate on the interior remodeling while the mechanical and electrical rough in proceeded.

The existing building needed some upgrades as well. Access was needed to the attic areas. My carpenters had a stairway and landing in place but that was just the tip of the iceberg. A walkway needed to be constructed throughout the entire attic space of the original building. This particular building was one of the original stone buildings erected in the late 1800's. At over a hundred years old, that would prove a real challenge. Jim Sorensen briefed me on the remodeling work performed in years past. Probably the most intense and most controversial had to be around the local bat population. Yes, I said BAT population.

Wyoming isn't known for its wide concentration of the nocturnal mammals but never the less, this particular building had housed an extensive population of bats. The extermination of the colony was only part of the problem. Bat guano (poop) was encountered throughout the attic spaces of the original building. The stench as well as the sanitation issues were a major concern. Jim had cleaned and sanitized the entire area but he hadn't been able to complete the task. Very careful instructions were given to those employees that opened up new un-sanitized portions of the building. I had quite a few Native American workers who refused to work under those conditions despite the safety equipment that they were given. But after close to a hundred gallons of the same stain blocker paint used by Jim Sorensen, the space was pronounced 'Safe' by the health department.

The utility rough-in went well throughout the new addition, but upgrading the existing facilities was a nightmare. Time and time again a different route was needed for water and power services to be extended. Jim's knowledge of the building and modern materials/methods proved invaluable. But his greatest benefit to the project came during the connection of the two structures.

The existing building was erected using a sandstone block that had been hauled in from a quarry not to far distance from the town. But the plans called for a twelve feet wide archway through the exterior wall of the original building. The existing sandstone block wall was carrying the roof load for the entire South roof line. Jim had a suggestion and as an engineer I was glad he was involved.

His design was a modified sandwich compressive configuration. Two Micro-Lam beams that measured 1 ½ inches thick would be connected through the stone wall using a series of Grade 8 one inch all thread bolts with locking nuts of both sides of the future header. Once these were in place then and only then could the existing sandstone be cut and removed one stone at a time. It took a considerable amount of time but it did work to perfection. The entire arch was then framed around and concealed from prying eyes. It was well thought out by all involved.

The sheetrock and taping took much longer than expected. Temporary heat was needed to provide the drying time for the perf-a-tape compound to dry. But the end job was first class. Then Jerry, the carpenter from Billings went to hanging doors. He was good, really good! He hung the entire array of doors in one weekend and he did it by himself. To this day, I do not know how he could handle a one hundred and fifty pound door without help. The task helped get back some of the time we had lost during the sheet rocking. The flooring crew from Billings was scheduled to arrive in two more weeks and all the cabinetry needed to be in place beforehand.

It took some over-time hours but all the base cabinets were installed. As the flooring was being laid, each room would receive countertops and specialty equipment in order. I didn't think that many pulls, brackets, curtains, and bumpers could possibly fit in each and every room but they did. The dental wing called for an epoxy-resin counter to be field installed. I didn't understand until it arrived by special delivery. It was jet black in color and weighed a ton. It weighed so much that it would need to be handled in four separate pieces.

The acid resistant quality needed in some dental work was designed into the dental lab. That counter was an item that I had never heard of let alone installed before. Since the base cabinetry was in place, the counters were arranged exactly where they would remain throughout their life expectancy. Each section was positioned with an eighth inch gap separating each one. The epoxy filler had been shipped separately from the tops and it was my responsibility to mix and complete this portion of the counter top.

I had used duct tape in defining joint thicknesses before, so I applied the same technique again. Both sides of the joint was taped precisely in place so as to not allow any of the filler material to migrate where it wasn't wanted. Then with all the joints properly taped and protected, I mixed the epoxy filler solution. I used a small margin trowel to work the epoxy into each seam and then with a different putty knife coated with turpentine I tooled the joints until they were slick and shiny. The set time of the epoxy filler was only fifteen minutes so I had to work efficiently and a s quick as possible to achieved the look needed. I was glad I had planned the whole process over and over in my mind because it worked to perfection!

The medical and dental equipment began to arrive along with technicians to install each and every piece. I was amazed at all the stainless steel used in each piece. We were getting close to crunch time with a grand opening having already been established. I hired a crew to clean the entire building the week before the final completion date. Busy B Cleaners claimed they were up to the challenge. (I hope so because my wife and daughters manned Busy B Cleaners.)

We furnished all the rags, cleaners, and buckets needed. When we stopped to pick up the commercial cleaning supplies, my wife asked why we had purchased so much stainless steel cleaner. My reply was, " Just wait until you see the equipment that you will be cleaning." And even then I still wondered if we had purchased enough.

Busy B Cleaners jumped right in and systematically deep cleaned each and every room from stem to stern. My only assignment was to stay out of the road and to keep the pizza and sodas coming. Quite frankly that wasn't the easiest of assignments . Fort Washakie isn't known for its wide assortment of pizza parlors. Lander was the closest source and it was a half hour away! But my assignment was completed even though the barbecue chicken pizza was hardly touched at all.

Just as a traveler drops down into Fort Washakie, there is a gigantic sign made out of white boulders, which reads F O R T. It probably measures fifty feet tall and sits up against a bluff overlooking the community. My daughters had noticed it the very first time we drove into Ft. Washakie. As we were leaving the job site following the cleaning of the new clinic, we noticed that some of the local youth had modified the huge sign. In place of the "O", they prankster had changed it to an "A". We all had a good chuckle at the finished product. (FART WASHAKIE)

SHOSHONI LDS REMODEL

During the closing days of the Ft.Washakie Clinic, I began looking for my next project. The LDS Branch in Shoshoni had grown enough to warrant an expansion. I discussed it with Stan at his office in Billings and obtained the bid documents in anticipation of

CONSTRUCTION HICCUPS

submitting a bid on the project. The date arrived and we were awarded the contract. We were "Cooking with Crisco" to use a popular phrase from Fremont County circles.

I had recently completed design and construction of a Pre-School building that was in need of exterior improvements. The immaculate sod at the Shoshoni church was there for the using. All we had to do was cut and transport it thirty miles. Call Triple L Trucking and a fifty foot trailer was filled to over-flowing. It took the better part of an entire Saturday to cut, load, transport, unload, and lay all that beautiful green sod. The cost was higher than anticipated but the Smart Start Academy had a backyard to use at their discretion.

During the course of removing the sod from the site in Shoshoni, I noticed the entire sub-grade moving. I can best equate it to driving the equipment across a gigantic bowl of jell-o. It would bob and wave in every possible direction due to the soils that had been exposed. I notified the Structural Engineer over the project. He was flabbergasted at what he was observing. I, in turn, was put upon to price out a change order to export the expansive soils off site and import a structural fill just as soon as possible.

Dave J, who was under contract to perform the excavation, was contacted and prices obtained. The next two weeks were consumed in removing and importing suitable materials. Inberg-Miller Engineers had a technician on-site each and every day to observe the delivery of the approved structural fill. Both daily logs and density testing was performed as load after load was spread and compacted in place. A change order is not the most advantageous way to begin a project. But both the Church representative and an independent testing agency approved the fill. The concrete work was ready to commence. Willie, Scott, Danny, Brian, Jess, and myself began forming and pouring in earnest in order to make up some ground lost during the soils change order. Things were going well and we were back on schedule having worked six days a week to achieve that. The footers and the stem walls were cast without incident. Dave J. began the backfill operations making sure to place the interior fill in equal proportions with the exterior backfill so as not to place any undo pressures on the green walls of the foundation. The building slab was set and John joint used to control the random cracking of the slab itself. My aluminum screed was approved the help place and consolidate the 6 bag concrete that would be delivered for a continuous pour of the 10,000 square foot addition. The pour day was set and all went as planned. It was rewarding to observe my crew performing the placement just like they had been trained to do. They even had time to laugh and rib each other about their personal activities over the past weekend. At the end of the day the slab was in place with saw cutting of the control joints to follow as soon as the concrete had hydrated enough the withstand the diamond saw blade.

Every contractor bids more jobs than he can possibly cover realizing that a few of those bids will come through and the majority will never materialize. I received a follow-up call from Fixter Construction about this same time. The Lander Clinic bid had been successful. Now what was I suppose to do? I notified Stan in Billings that I would not be able to complete the LDS Church remodel in Shoshoni and the concrete work was completely done as per the subcontract agreement. He would send a replacement just as soon as possible. The Lander Medical Clinic was breaking ground sooner than expected.

LANDER MEDICAL CLINIC

I worked out a transition plan that would span the next two weeks and sent my crew to Lander to begin the formwork on the two-story dental remodel (It had the potential to cover my expenses throughout the winter months.) The Lander Medical Clinic sets on a hill overlooking the Middle Fork of the Popo Agie River. The plan called for a two-story expansion between the existing building and the river itself. The access to the new addition would be extremely tight and then there was the river to contend with.

This project was the first time I was confronted with the Federal Clean Water Act. It had multiple aspects that would directly influence this and many similar projects of its kind. Fixter Construction was responsible to prepare a plan, which would satisfy all the requirements of this mandate. A Storm Water Protection Plan (SWPP) was prepared and submitted for approval through the Federal Department of Environmental Quality (DEQ). They approved it and I had to implement each and every provision of that plan.

The basic premise of the plan was to prevent storm water from entering the existing river before it could be cleaned and/or treated to a quality that is higher than the waters of the river. Any sediment, oils, or other contaminants had to be removed from the rain or snow melt before it was allowed to drain into the Popo Agie River. A new addition to the existing parking lot was designed into this SWPP along with the street and parking facilities already in use. Curb cuts and diversion barricades needed to be constructed as well as a holding lagoon at the bottom of the bank right next to the river. An erosion structure also was to be incorporated to control the storm water as it flowed from the parking lot towards this new lagoon where the contaminants could be deposited before the water was released into the river..

The use of temporary 'Waddles' (porous tubes filled with straw) were to be used during the construction phase to accomplish the same thing that the permanent devices would upon completion. A Silt Fence was installed to stop any infiltration onto the property from outside sources. The government had developed a very detailed set of standards that needed to be followed exactly during the installation, maintenance, and removal of the temporary devices. And of course monthly inspection reports had to be filed with all of the necessary agencies involved.

The key to the success of this design was a reinforced concrete trough installed at the lowest point of the parking facility and then dropping two hundred feet down the steep slope towards the waiting lagoon. This chute had to restrict the flow of all storm waters and prevent any erosion of the steep side slope in the process. The design was quite simple but the implementation was a completely different story.

An eighteen inch curb cut was needed to direct the storm water flow down the incline. At that point a three foot wide concrete trough was poured from the top extending downhill a good two hundred feet. Periodically along this chute, we hand set numerous boulders of varying sizes and profiles directly in the path of the cascading run-off. This not only slowed the waters but provided an artistically pleasing feature not previously in place. This entire project involved a tremendous amount of hand labor and improvised tools. We ended up using five gallon buckets to transport the concrete from the top of the parking area throughout the length of the two chutes that the Civil Engineer identified. The amount of concrete needed was minor compared to the man-hours used throughout. The final outcome was both attractive and DEQ friendly.

The footing layout was somewhat unusual due to an elevator shaft being located almost dead center in the new addition. I had worked on some elevator designs while in Cody but they had been framed in using steel studs and this design consisted in concrete walls and floor. Our work would have to be precise with very little margin for error. We double checked every measurement and squared every corner especially those of the elevator system.

The day before the footing pour, I scheduled a pre-pour conference with all of the personnel involved. I also invited the concrete supplier and the testing agency. We went through every possible scenario making sure everybody involved knew what was expected of them during the pour. Since a concrete pump was going to be used, a lot of the discussion centered around the pump location, arrival, priming, and clean up.

I turned to the testing technician and asked him point blank," Where do you plan on taking your samples?" When he answered, " Directly from the mixer." The fur began to fly. The pumper claimed that the mix would lose at least an inch of slump as it passed through the pump lines. The supplier interjected his experience with the mix design. If the slump is increased after it arrives on the job site then they are not responsible for the integrity of the final product. After each had voiced their position, Dave, the project superintendent, was able to develop a mutual agreement with every party in attendance. The concrete would be delivered to the job site at a five- inch slump, the testing of the air content and cylinders would happen as the concrete leaves the trunk of the pump truck, and no water was to be added to the mix except by Dave himself. And with that agreement the pour was set for 7 A.M. the next day.

My crew did not have a ton of experience around concrete pump trucks. But once the concrete was in the forms they knew exactly what to do. So I agreed to man the trunk of the pump truck. I reviewed briefly my simple hand signals I had always used on hundreds of pours and we were all ready to begin. I felt it important to start out on the slower side of the pumps capabilities and then progress from there. It was a good thing too. The pump became plugged during the first five minutes of the pour.

Each section of the pump hose had to be dis-mantled one by one until the plug was located. At that point the pump operator turned to Dave and requested a higher slump or the same result could be expected throughout the day. Dave turned to the mixer driver and requested that five gallons be added to the load. My experience reassured me that the slump would be increased about a half inch and the compressive strength would drop by a hundred pounds. The pump lines were reconnected and the pour proceeded from there. It is amazing that a mere five gallons of water could affect the pumpability of the mix but seeing is believing.

The remaining three mixers arrived with the slight increase in water content and the pour continued without further mishaps. But we still had the walls to pour as well as the entire basement slabs on grade.

The foundation walls were designed to stand ten feet tall. Fixter had agreed to furnish the Symons forms and my crew all had some experience with the pins and dogs used in ganging these forms together. Again the exactness needed in the layout was crucial. We snapped the concrete lines with extra care and then decided to shoot down a 2 x 4 plate that would serve as a stabilizing start to the wall formwork. I had recently purchased a Ramset powder actuated gun that we would use to drive the concrete pins through the wood into the footing concrete. We had to sort through a trailer full of 2 x 4's in order to locate enough straight lumber to ensure the detail needed for all the walls.

The next four days were spent erecting form after form in place and on top of each other to match the structural drawings in every aspect. The Symons system we were using required all the rebar be in place before the forms could be installed. We were not journeymen rod-busters but we did know how to accomplish the task even if it took just a little longer. Again the forms were in place and the next concrete pour was scheduled for the following day.

Again the concrete arrived at 7 A.M. with everybody ready for the day's work. Having learned a few things from our first pour, we were able to complete the entire pour well before darkness over took us. The pump, the mixers, the vibrators, and testing agency all worked to perfection. We could all sleep well and return on Monday ready to strip the forms.

As we were chatting about the Monday's tasks, somebody asked a troubling question. "How are we going to get the forms that are inside the foundation out of the hole once stripped?" We all looked at each other with a look of total disbelief. Up and until that very moment, we had not even thought it would be a problem. But due to the tightness of the job site and impossibility in getting equipment around the perimeter, it was to prove a very unplanned for consequence. As the owner and head lead man on the crew, I just let it out. " I guess we will just have to take them over the top then!"

We planned our attack with three men positioned strategically on the areas to be stripped. One man on the inside of the wall, another on top of the wall, and a third man on the outside to receive the panel as it was man- handled over the top of the ten foot high concrete wall. It took a couple of tries until each man was able to master what he needed to accomplish. We all had agreed to take turns ay each post until the entire task was completed.

Everything went as planned until it was my turn to work on top of the wall and swing the concrete form from the one side of the wall around to the outside and down to the man loading the pallet. We were moving along nicely until we neared the inside corner of the foundation. In order to pass off the panel from the inside to the outside I would need to walk a few steps along the wall and then hand off the panel to the man located there.

The first couple of panels were handled smoothly and correctly but I must have been distracted because on the very next sequence I lost my balance. The panel and I both dropped out of sight on the backside of that ten-foot high wall. I do not remember much about the crash landing but somehow I managed to land away from the panel itself. After a heated Scotch blessing I grabbed that panel and heaved it up and over the wall! I didn't even stop to think if anybody was in the road of that flying concrete panel. I was mad at myself for losing my balance and not being smart enough to have planned for a better method of panel extraction from the inside of that foundation.

Towards the tail end of removing all the concrete panels, the success of a job nearly completed began to take hold of my crew. They were excited to have the walls all poured and were in the last stages of loading the panels for return shipment. Four of my crew decided to ride the empty forklift back down the hill they had been transporting panels up all day long. They all jumped on as the ole' forklift began to gain speed down the incline. Willie was driving and he hollers out, "The brakes are going out!"

The three men that had jumped on for a free ride, Scott, Danny, and Jesse all bailed off to safety leaving Willie to his fate. Without any brakes whatsoever, Willie manages to point the forklift straight towards a tangle of river birch that separated the river from the streambed. Kerwump! The forklift nose-dived into the briar patch of tangled birch wood and native grasses. The forklift was stopped less than four feet from a watery demise and Willie only received a few minor scratches. They remaining crew came sprinting down the bank to help where needed. Once they had found everything in sound order, they began howling with delight and continued right on laughing for the next couple of hours. They were extremely lucky that afternoon and they knew it.

The floors of the lower level were our next milestone. But the grading, electrical and plumbing work needed to be completed before we could pour the interior floor. While these items were being completed, we set about forming and pouring sidewalks and perimeter steps for complete access around the three exposed sides of the addition. Our goal was to perform all the exterior landscaping before the winter months set in. As each façade received the appropriate concrete work the topsoil was graded to spec and planting beds and trees followed in close pursuit. The entire perimeter had a twelve-foot walkway that was touching the concrete walls we had just recently poured. It was taking shape nicely.

With all the lower level utilities in place the concrete pump was scheduled back to the clinic. We decided to pour the basement slab in three pours to help with placing efforts and to minimize cracking. Except for the elevator shaft the floor was one enormous span of flatwork. The two bathrooms were held out for a later pour to allow for floor drains and the ceramic floor to be recessed. My aluminum screed was used for the majority of the screeding operations but like usual a few smaller pieces needed to be hand rodded to tie everything together. The slabs were completed just in time as the steel bar joists arrived right on schedule.

The floor system was centered around the center elevator shaft. Weld plates had been cast into the wall sections to provide the attachment necessary for each of the steel joists. Once these were welded in place the 20 gage steel decking was then welded to all the spanning joists. The concrete pump was then called in for one last job. The specifications called for a lightweight concrete structural slab to be poured on top of the steel deck system. I think we totally wore out a couple of sets of power trowel blades on those slabs we poured that year.

My contract was all but complete and my crew had all headed back to school and their professions when John Fixter approached me with an urgent request. He had over booked his own crews and he needed somebody to take over the supervision of the remaining work at the clinic we were working on! I could easily be committed for the rest of the winter and into the early spring season. I was totally amazed at how things always seemed to have a way of working out for the best.

The steel stud framers were well on their way and the utility crews were right on their tails with the rough-in work. The roof trusses were expected within the month and I started getting calls from the roofer under contract about when he could start. Dave had left me a well planned out itinerary for the next two months.

The building was progressing as good as can be expected when all of a sudden out of the blue I received notice that the sheetrock company that Fixter had lined out to hang, tape, and texture the walls had declared bankruptcy. John and I began to scramble. We needed a sub-contractor and immediately. Finally after close to a month of scouring the state, John signed a contractor from Casper to complete the job. The framing had been completed and the exterior masonry was in place now with the utilities all roughed in the sheetrock work was the link in the schedule that had to be closed.

I was a little taken back when a crew of five men showed up to hang all the sheetrock on both levels. I could envision four or five crews that size needed to catch up for the lost time. But as I watched and observed, a glimmer of hope appeared. These guys were paid by the sheet and not by the hour. They knew what they were doing and the semi loads of sheetrock began to disappear on a regular basis.

The second week after they had begun hanging the lower level a cold front moved into the valley and it promised to hang around for a while. The hangers continued right on hanging at a torrid pace but I received a visit from their taping foreman shortly there after. As he walked throughout the freshly hung rooms, he would place his hand on the surface of each and every wall. Upon completion of his walk through, he informed me that the walls were too cold for his taping crew to work efficiently and I had a week to fix the problem. I promptly notified John Fixter of their inspection and asked for help.

That very week a rental outfit from Casper delivered two one million BTU propane fired heaters to the job site along with a dozen box fans to help move air around the building. A heater was placed on each level along with a 500-gallon propane tank to fuel the large external heaters. All I had to do was seal up the doorways where these two heaters were sitting and keep the propane tanks full. The tanks were rentals from a local propane vendor who would check on the levels daily and keep them above the 50% mark continuously.

When the taping foreman returned that next week, he conducted his same walk through as he had before. He turned to me and exclaimed; " Now that is what I'm talking about!" He promptly called in two taping crews to begin on separate floors bright and early in the morning. They showed up with a flatbed loaded to the gills with box after box of taping compound and perf-a–tape.

They all looked totally wasted from the lack of sleep but went straight to work unloading the two trailers of materials and supplies. I was introduced to each of the crew foremen and I showed them where fresh water could be drawn from and where they could set up their mixing operation. And without so much as a howdy hoe they spilt into two crews and began taping.

The electrician was nearly complete with his outlet rough in and as previously directed had a live outlet in every single room. The tapers each had a halogen lamp that he carried from room to room to satisfy his need for well lit walls. I also noticed that each crew had one man that did all their mixing. He was very particular as to the consistency and arrangement of his mixing station. He had to be because the tapers were consuming the taping compound (Mud) like it was candy. Just as soon as he had a five-gallon bucket ready a taper showed up and away it went. I saw the very latest taping tools put to good use. Bazookas, banjos, mud boxes, and hawks were all well used by the crews. I also noticed that each taper had his own array of taping knives in every width imaginable. They were fun to watch.

As each room was being completed, I asked why they weren't applying any texture to the walls so my painters could begin. They informed me that their "texture truck" would be here on Saturday. They had to be on another job come Monday. They weren't the Texture crew anyway. I wasn't concerned about working Saturday since we had been working most Saturdays anyways but I had only seen men using spray hoppers and that would take a lot longer than one day to texture the entire building.

But that Friday a masking crew arrived and began the detail oriented task of masking frames, windows, cabinetry, and anything else that wasn't scheduled to receive an' Orange Peel' texture the following day. Sure enough at 7 A.M. a two-ton truck arrived carrying a 300 gallon tank which was ¾ full of mixed texture compound. A quick walk through by the lead man and a decision to start on the lower level was made. By the time that level was textured, the masking crew would have the main level completed. And away they went dragging multiple sections of hose with them. They started in the hardest to reach places and textured their way back towards the two-ton truck. It was obvious that they had applied texture for years. The evenness and quality of their work was totally amazing to watch. By one o'clock they had the basement level completed. The humidity level on that level must have been in the high 90's.

They took a short lunch break while the masking crew gathered up their tools and clutter. Then they were at it again. Room by room they worked their way down each and every hallway. As the clock struck 7 P.M. they were applying texture to the alcove that would serve as the main entry to the new clinic. If I hadn't seen it with my own two eyes, I wouldn't have believed it could be done. The painters were called and given the green light to begin painting on Monday morning. All of the masking was left in place thus eliminating the need to re-mask everything again.

The paint color scheme was a saving grace of sorts. With all those walls and ceilings to receive paint, the architect and designer whittled it down to two tones. The public access areas would receive a muted tan color and the examination/work areas were designated to receive an off-white color. This would allow more versatility in artworks and cabinetry detailing. The painters were ready to blow through all those rooms. They brought two airless sprayers onto the job. The two sprayers were kept busy from morning to night applying a primer and then two coats of a high-end latex paint. The entire building interior was completed in five days and that included the removal of all the masking papers and tape left by the texturing crew.

With the painting completed, the next step was to lay the underlayment on the concrete floor. Most commercial buildings just use the concrete floor as its own underlayment, but this architect wanted a sound barrier between the lower basement and the main floor where the patients would be taken care of. The architect specified a product that I was not familiar with at all. Gyp-Crete has gypsum, sand, and cement blended together to an almost liquid consistency. The gypsum helps keep the cracking to a minimum as well as reduce the transmission of sound through the floor.

The company that applied the Gyp-Crete came from Denver. They arrived with the pumping equipment, cement, and the gypsum. Fixter needed to provide masonry sand and a small crew to feed the sand into their hopper before it was mixed with the other ingredients. So I stepped in as a laborer for the day, and helped shovel masonry sand for the better part of a day.

I did get to observe the lay-down operation too. It was an operation completely different from what I expected. The lay down crew all strapped on studded boots. They were actually metal soles that had removable studs spaced a half inch apart both ways. The studs used varied from job to job depending on the thickness desired. The clinic was to receive a one inch underlayment throughout the main floor area. So the crew all secured one inch studs to their platform soles and began pumping the underlayment. They also had tined racks set to the depth of one inch. As the Gyp-Crete was pumped into the building, the crew simply spread the liquid product flat using the tined rakes. The liquid nature of the underlayment allowed it to seek a flat finished surface with just a little effort. The tines on the rakes and the studs on their boots kept the product flat throughout. The hydration of the underlayment took the longest care. Nobody was allowed on the floors for 48 hours. The final product was extremely flat and durable making it perfect for this application.

Finally the finish trim work could begin in earnest. Drop ceilings were needed in those rooms that did not have sheetrock ceilings.

Specialty apparatus was needed in every exam room. Movable curtains needed to be installed once the ceiling grid was in place. And the two semi-loads of cabinetry that had been stored off-site could now be unloaded and stitched together. Fixter had contracted with a Salt Lake cabinetmaker to work on this intricate detail of the clinic.

They fabricated each and every piece of wood trim and cabinetry for the entire building. Their contract included the installation work too. But Fixter was responsible for the transportation costs to get all the oak from Salt Lake to Lander. As each piece was completed at the mill in Sandy, it was bundled and labeled before tightly packing it in two fifty-five foot enclosed trailers. These two trailers had been setting adjacent to the new addition for the past month awaiting the green light to unload.

A detailed master list was in hand as we began sorting through the menagerie of oak trim, countertops, and base cabinets contained in those trailers. Each room had an identifying number, which corresponded to a coded tag on each piece of oak. What we thought would only take a couple of days in turn stretched out over the next three weeks. The systematic loading of the finished product was not systematic at all. It was more like an act of desperation as every piece was crammed into the trailers at the last second before the drivers were scheduled to leave. But room by room finally filled up as we checked off each and every piece from the inventory sheets. I guess I was a little surprised to actually find every single item on the packing slip from the mill in Sandy.

The mill sent out two crews of finish carpenters to begin the stitching together of the materials in each individual room. Some rooms were quite simple. A base cabinet, counter top, a top cabinet and 4 inch base molding for the perimeter in each of the exam rooms. The lab, kitchen and reception areas were quite definitely more elaborate. The shop drawings for each room really were well put together. And I was grateful that multiple sets of each had been mailed separately. The finish carpenters were great when it came to working with wood but their paper work was a nightmare. They lost more sheets to the drawings than I thought humanly possible. But slowly and surely each and every room was completed and signed off.

Before I would release the Salt Lake crew from the job site, I held a walk through for the owners and the architects. They seemed quite pleased as I was at the final product. They went over each and every room with a fine-tooth comb. A punch list of items was generated and it was only two pages long---a miracle in and of itself! I was especially pleased at the design and fabrication of the main reception desk. It was nearly twelve feet long and incorporated fluted oak paneling, fabric in-fills, and miscellaneous mirrors throughout. It was very pleasing to the eye and just seemed to draw the public right to the front of it. The oak work combined with computer terminals, power bars, and switchboard hardware was well thought out and installed very professionally.

The clinic staff were getting anxious to move in and begin see patients in our yet to be completed addition. I was asked by John Fixter, when I thought the remodeling could be completed. I thought through all the details still left to be completed and gave him a date about a month out. He wasn't in agreement and he asked if that time line could be cut in half? I stated that working weekends and overtime could yield that goal. He looked me straight in the eye and simply stated, " Then let's make it happen!" I had two maybe two and a half weeks to wind up the loose ends of the remodel. The sub- contractors were not excited at all because they knew all of the steps needed to complete each task. But everybody decided to give it their best shot.

Every corner of each floor had some type of work that needed to be completed. Electricians, plumbers, Division ten specialties, ceiling tile , and flooring installers were working double shifts. The architect was making daily visits to the building claiming that he was there to check on the quality of the workmanship. I am sure he didn't just want things thrown together at the last minute. But he finally divulged the real reason for his vigil. His comment to me was, " It is like watching time lapsed photography. Every time I walk through the doors, the interior has noticeably changed."

So much had developed that I was able to invite the Busy B Cleaners back for the final cleaning of many of the rooms. I accused then of just playing on the elevator when every time I saw one of them it was either going into or coming out of those double doors. Buckets of cleaning supplies were definitely vanishing as they followed the carpet layers and electricians down each and every hallway.

Once again the cleaners cleaned up more pizza than I thought humanly possible. But come to find out they were distributing soda and pizza to every single soul in the building. But if that was all it took to keep the workers on site to complete their specific tasks, it was money well spent. And with the architect making daily inspections, the punch list was also dissolving right before our eyes. The certificate of occupancy was granted while the employees were being trained on the new equipment that had been purchased and installed. The Lander Medical Clinic was completed and turned over to the owners!

ARAPAHO CLINIC

I didn't need to wait long for my next project. Fixter Construction was awarded a contract to expand the facilities at another Indian Health Service clinic. This clinic was a bit closer to home since it was in Arapaho on the East side of the Wind River Indian Reservation. Fixter decided to use Skyline for the entire addition both as a concrete/carpentry sub-contractor and as a Manager to oversee the subs that he had enlisted. It would be a pleasure working with Jim Sorensen again as the Indian Health Service Engineer.

The existing clinic was approximately 10,000 square feet and had been in service for the past twenty years. The staff and equipment were excited to finally get the expansion they so desperately needed. The addition would double the square footage as well as upgrade their service potential. By adding new equipment and technology the Arapaho people would now be able to receive the local examinations and consultations that in years past required then to travel off the reservation. The fees were always higher and the average trip to a major hospital was at least 300 miles one way.

The plan was quite simple and maximized the square footage costs. It was to be added directly south of the existing building and would utilize a common wall. Access into the new addition would be through one of three hallways that would penetrate the existing exterior wall. The main entrance would also be enlarged and allow entrance into both wings of the clinic. The roof of the addition would be constructed as a completely independent part of the new addition with a walkway cut into the existing parapet enclosure. The exterior façade of both would be upgraded using natural occurring stone from the reservation and a parking lot that was almost three times as large as the present area.

Every effort to utilize local Indian owned companies was put into play. Evans Excavation would be performing all of the grading, paving, and excavation work since they were Indian owned and hired almost entirely Indian help. Their equipment and manpower were up to date and well maintained too. I can still remember that first day of digging.

It was during the first dozen buckets of excavation that some bones appeared in the track hoe hopper. Of course, the local business office of the Arapaho Tribe was call out immediately. A thorough investigation ensued with the tribal elders being the first men called. But the only bones that were unearthed were of a large dog with nothing human being identified. I sighed a huge sigh of relief. I really didn't want the job shut down indefinitely while a Federal Archeologist investigated the remains.

Doug Evans was a member of past business councils for the tribe and was quite excited that his crew could continue digging. Within a weeks time the proper gravel strata was identified and the new parameters were open and ready for the concrete work. It was a basic footing foundation plan with nothing different or innovative to cause a slow down. I had made a few Indian friends while working in Ft. Washakie and I promptly notified the Oldman brothers when I needed employees. The TERO Officer in Ft. Washakie didn't seem be that interested in hiring her family members to work on the Arapaho side of the reservation. Ronnie and his brothers were eager and qualified to fill all my needs during the construction of the footers and stemwall. An additional footing was cast along the entire length of the building and exactly half way between the existing foundation and the proposed exterior wall of the new clinic. The span from outside of wall to the common wall was too long for the Trus-Joist system to meet the load requirements of the equipment and people to be using the clinic.

The foundation work moved along nicely as well as the treated lumber pony wall construction. An option to pour six foot foundation walls was thrown out due to costs. A four-foot stemwall with a twelve inch footer would give them five feet of head clearance which would just have to be enough. The only issue that surfaced was with the electrician. Rocky Mountain Electric had been hired as a local subcontractor. When asked about tying in the electrical grounding wire to the new reinforcement, he informed me that the existing ground rod would be more than enough to do the job. And since a state electrical inspector was needed for every single inspection, I allowed the ground rod issue to slide through. (I would regret this decision in the not too distant future) But the floor sheathing was on and the walls were going up quicker than anybody expected.

The roof trusses weren't scheduled to be delivered for another three weeks. I placed a call to the truss yard to see if a quicker delivery was possible. They said they would do what they could but weren't promising anything. The framing crew was clipping along at a good pace and would have all the walls completed and the sheathing on within the week. After scouring the plans I finally identified some work to tide them over until the trusses could be delivered. I decided to begin demolishing the existing façade in preparation for the masons to begin setting the stone work along the new exterior. The south wall of the clinic would be exposed to the weather but the forecast for the next month was favorable. So off it came while watching the weather forecast daily. Who ever said that construction wasn't without risks?

The new trusses were delivered as promised and I had a crane there to unload them. The profile of the truss was different than any I had set before. The roof pitch was only a 1/12 pitch but these trusses had the parapet walls attached. The design was different but the crane operator and my erection crew were ready for anything. I had planned on using the crane for two solid days during the erection process but things went so well we released the crane at the end of the first day. The trusses were in place ready for the roof sheathing.

That next week was spent laying the plywood sheathing over the entire roof and that included the parapet sheathing as well. The framing inspection passed without any trouble at all. It was time to dry in the roof and begin the utility rough-in. The entire process was flowing as smooth as glass. I for the state electrical and mechanical inspections since the county jurisdiction does not include reservation construction. I didn't anticipate any trouble at all, but was I ever in for a surprise.

The mechanical and plumbing rough in inspections went just fine but the electrical inspector spent two solid days at the job site. He called a special inspection review board in on the third day to hand me a Red Tag for the entire building and the IHS inspector that was in attendance proceeded to sot down the entire facility! Apparently the whole grounding methodology was placing everyone there in danger of electrocution!

As the facility was being evacuated, the review board along with Rocky Mountain Electric's owner and head electrician met to discuss the remedy to the problems. I thought it was very advantageous to have an approved solution to begin working on immediately, but the head electrician just wanted to argue. John Fixter was in attendance and finally just told the electrician to complete the extras or a new electrician would be hired to correct the glaring issues. The electrician did agree to do the work but only because the state board would pull his license if he didn't. Needless to say that severed any cooperation between Fixter and Rocky Mountain Electric from that point forward. As the superintendent on this project, I was left to pick up the pieces. The State Electrical Board also placed Rocky Mountain Electric and each of their electricians on probation for failure to comply with the National Electric Code along with a substantial fine. They would use the monies associated with the probation to pay for a bi-weely inspection of each of their ongoing projects (the Arapaho Clinic was not their only active project).

I was still under a huge burden to try and oversee the electrical work at the clinic. I possessed only a very elementary knowledge of the trade and would be relying on the bi-weekly inspections quite heavily. But the first thing was to get the system grounding up to code. A trench needed to be dug a least three foot deep. Two strands of rebar had to be cast the entire length of this trench with a copper grounding cable connecting this reinforced trench to the main electrical disconnect of the building. Only when this was completed and signed off by the state inspector, could the clinic be reopened for business. Wow! What an ordeal to be put through!

But after a week of intensive excavation, rebar, and concrete work the clinic was re-opened for the tribe to take full advantage of. That next week was really something to behold. The Arapahoe people were really dependent on this clinic for their medical necessities. Every thing from daily prescriptions to sports physicals to emergency room services were provided free of charge to all tribal members. They could travel into Riverton to receive this same care but they would end up paying for the treatments just like everyone else. But the IHS and the BIA had passed a resolution that stipulated that in order to receive the free medical and dental services they were used to receiving they had to request these items at the home reservations. That pretty well forced the average Native American back to the place of his birth. So much for expanding their horizons and rising above the traditions they had grown up with or any higher education possibilities.

One item that was definitely included in the renovation and expansion plans was to eliminate the exterior access to the crawl space under the floor. A locking access hatch was included in the flooring design and was to be located near the center of the new foundation. An incident occurred that really punctuated the conditions that exist on the reservation.

Shortly before the exterior access was to be closed permanently, we received some over night visitors. They had obviously staked out the site beforehand because they knew exactly where to gain access into the clinic. They had jerry-rigged the exterior access door so they could enter by means of the crawl space. Then once they were under the floor, they headed straight for the new floor hatch. Their next step after gaining access to the main floor of the existing building was to let themselves into the Pharmacy Section.

An emergency inventory revealed that a substantial supply of pharmacy strength pain killers were missing! They also helped themselves to several cases of cough syrup (probably for the alcohol contained in the brew) and on their way out they robbed the stash of quarters near the vending machines. The workers at the clinic had no definite way of knowing the quantity of quarters missing but estimated it to be around $300.

The drugs were of an intensity and quantity to really cause some serious damage to people who did not know how to distribute then. But the really crazy thing about the theft was the quarters. Instead of laying low and restricting the use of all those quarters, they proceeded to a local bank on the very next day following the robbery to cash them in. The cashier alertly contacted the bank management when over a thousand quarters were presented for exchange by two Indian males. They were apprehended less than twenty four hours following the break-in. They should have been included on an episode of America's Dumbest Criminals for the whole debaucher.

The warmer weather allowed both the exterior site work to proceed along with the interior finishes. Both had sufficient equipment and manpower to keep each area on schedule. I was helping out inside the dental suite one day when a cry was heard from outside the front entry. "There's a Tornado!" I waited a few minutes while everyone else crowded outside and then I stepped out the front door.

Sure enough off to the East along the highway to the Gas Hills a funnel cloud was visible. It had touched down and was headed straight towards Arapaho! The air outside was a clammy calm sort of feeling different than anything I have ever experienced. As I stood transfixed at the sight, I heard several tribal members gasp as they headed for their vehicles. I was sure they were headed to their homes' to button down the hatches ' so to speak. But no sooner had they left the parking lot, I saw the clouds open up and the funnel lifted up and disappeared right into the cloud bank that was as dark and foreboding as any I have seen. The remainder of the day my crew kept a wary eye peeled towards that spot, but the excitement was over and done with. I was pleased to see that phenomenon.

The building was progressing on schedule and the parking lot was ready to begin when I received a phone call stating that the curb and gutter work needed to be postponed for three weeks. I couldn't believe it. I called Fixter right back and suggested that the Oldman Brothers could do the concrete work using my forms. John jumped at the opportunity. I had one hundred feet of steel curb and gutter forms but the radius forms would need to be site built. I ordered enough lap siding to satisfy the footage needed. I also ordered a couple hundred steel stakes from Casper Concrete to be delivered first thing in the morning!

And by first thing in the morning I mean by 6 A.M. Over the years I had developed a relationship with the manager of the DLR Freight Depot. He allowed me to pick up freight at his depot in Riverton directly off the Denver semi that stopped daily. All I had to do was get the items back loaded on the truck and then be there by six to receive the order. It had saved me countless hours and frustration. The assorted steel stakes were all palletized and I was johnny on the spot to sidetrack the shipment.

The Oldman Brothers, Ronnie, Melvin, and Joe; had hours of experience with concrete formwork including hand setting miles of curb and gutter. By the time I arrived with the extra stakes needed they had the first hundred feet of straightaway set and ready for the pour. They spent the next six hours constructing jigs and Masonite formwork to complete the first of dozens inside and outside radius pours. Concrete was ordered for 6 A.M. the following morning.

The first ten yards of 6 bag concrete arrived on schedule and the site work crew of six Native Americans went right to work. It became evident after just twenty minutes that they knew what they were doing. The site engineer sighed a deep sigh of relief. He had expressed definite anxiety about the use of locals to pour the complicated curb and gutter work. The curb cuts and even the handicap ramps were handled with every bit of professionalism that I had seen around the area. Within the next two weeks the entire exterior concrete work was completed. The pavers were notified and paving would proceed as scheduled.

Jim Sorensen continued to make periodic visits both to monitor our progress and to ensure the best quality workmanship was followed. As the cabinetry was being installed, he let me in on a little secret. During the work at the Ft. Washakie Clinic he had been double ordering selected pieces of equipment knowing all along that they would be needed here in Arapaho. Now was the time for delivery. The equipment had been placed in storage awaiting the appropriate time for its delivery. Jim informed me that Shoshone Enterprises had been commissioned for the packing and delivery of the items from the Fort. Pending the arrival of the installation technicians, he would have the convoy delivered.

That following Wednesday was the agreed upon delivery date. The technicians had arrived that Monday and were busy connecting and testing the newer pieces of equipment. I was not prepared for the convoy of trailers that showed up from Shoshone Enterprises. I am certain every pickup and trailer in their fleet was on my job site. I recognized several of their operators since they had worked on and off again with me on the first clinic. They knew hoe expensive each piece of equipment was and handled everything with the upmost care. The problem came in where to store all that high end equipment until the technicians could get at it. I wanted each piece as close to its final resting place as possible but not too close as to inhibit the workers. Every piece either had a complete plastic covering or was still in a cardboard shipping container. Richard the manager of the Shoshone Enterprises even showed up to inventory every piece. (I honestly think he was there to inspect the building and compare it to

CONSTRUCTION HICCUPS

the one in Fort Washakie) By the end of the day, each and every item was accounted for and under lock and key!

The very next day I ordered an additional dumpster to handle all of the cardboard and plastic wrap that would be removed from all that equipment. I swear I was calling every other day for the dumpsters to be hauled away and be replaced with an empty one. But at the end of the month, the place was actually starting to look like a clinic instead of a distribution terminal. The detail work in each room was nearing completion and all the equipment had been installed and run through its operating cycle several times. The clinic staff were scheduled in to receive their training on each and every detail. Many of the staff from Ft. Washakie came over to assist and train the new staff.

It was time for the final cleaning of the Arapaho Clinic. And guess who got the call. Busy B Cleaners, front and center! I expected the building to be cleaned in half the time than the other clinics since it was half as big. But when my wife looked at the mess she informed me that this last one was twice as dirty as the first two. Her remark was appropriate," Don't your workers know how to clean up after themselves?" They recruited a couple od extra cleaners and headed right for the dirtiest spot on the whole site. The crawl space.

The ladies all had two large garbage bags tied to their belts and dust masks all around. Like real troopers they dove into the mess of insulation, 2x4's, garbage of every form and color, and spider webs everywhere. They were very systematic about the whole thing. As each cleaner filled another garbage bag, they drug it to the new access door where it was removed and an empty bag exchanged. Bag after bag was hoisted out through that hole in the floor and wheeled out to a waiting 30 cy dumpster. By the end of that first night they had completely filled the dumpster and I swear I never heard a single scream even though I was sure a friendly spider was uncovered more than once. But hey, the worst part was over...on to the main floor!

After another stop at the cleaning supply store the ambitious crew returned for another night of detailing and sanitizing. They really earned their pizza that night. Room after room and cabinet after cabinet was sterilized and left in perfect condition. By eight o'clock they were practically done. They would have been finished by ten o'clock if that vacuum cleaner belt hadn't failed them. I wasn't at all surprised when the spare belt arrived from home along with a half dozen Frostys fro the local Wendy's along with some French fries to dip the chocolate ice cream from the cup into eager hungry mouths. The project was complete by 11 P.M. that evening as everybody headed home for a shower and their very own beds.

At the final walk-through with the architect and the business council, several people commented on the cleanliness of the new clinic. But who ever heard of a final punch list that doesn't have a few items that need correction or completion. The Arapaho Clinic was no different than any other renovation project. But inside of a weeks time frame the punch list was completed. On his way out the door, John Washakie walked over to me and asked if I would come see him in Ft. Washakie that next Friday? A time was set and I was left to wonder about it for the next three days!

CONSTRUCTION MANAGER FOR SHOSHONE ENTERPRISES

I walked into John Washakie's office early that Friday not having a clue what he had in mind. John was a direct descendant of Chief Washakie and the President of the Shoshone Business Council. He was an easy man to talk with and he quickly put me at ease. He began by giving me a brief glimpse into the future of the Eastern Shoshone Tribe. It was refreshing to meet a Native American that was more concerned about what was happening in the next five years than in just what was happening in the next five days. He then look straight at me and asked if I would work for the Tribe during the next two years?

After a few hours of barter back and forth, I walked out of his office as the new Estimator for Shoshone Enterprises. I was both leery and excited all at the same time. We had talked about some upcoming projects and he wanted me to train somebody to take over my duties as estimator by the end of my employment. As I was driving home that day, it hit me that the duration of my contract with the Business Council and the increased salary that I would receive matched almost identical to the costs and time associated with my son's mission call to Tucson, Arizona. Coincidence? I don't think so!

I had met Richard Ferris on several occasions since he was the manager of Shoshone Enterprises. He was well liked by the employees and trusted by the Business Council. We spent the first day meeting employees and tribal personnel that I would be working with. Many I recognized from work on the clinic and refereeing basketball. I couldn't help but notice how lacking the employees were in both tools and know-how as I walked through the few building projects they were winding up. As we returned to the office, Dick turned to me and point blank asked," We need more work and you are the man we have hired to locate it."

I reviewed with him some of the leads I had been watching. The Washakie Dam Reconstruction will not begin until next spring. The BIA Scattered home-sites is still a good year out. The Arapaho Tribal Complex in Ethete is still in design. The repaving of the Ethete Highway has been postponed. He did not have any leads other than the ones I had pointed out. So I was basically starting from scratch.

It seemed like every day a few calls would come into the office from tribal members that needed their road cleared or some backhoe work etc. Dick and his core crew of operators always handled these calls promptly. I was set up with a computer and given access to the company employee records. At first glance, I noticed the pay scale of all the employees was a good 5-10 % above what I was used to seeing around Riverton and Lander. That was going to make it that much harder to land future work due to higher labor rates. But I had an idea. All Federal, State, and BIA projects stipulated that Davis-Bacon wage rates were to be used in the bidding process. That would help put all the bidders on the same page as far as labor costs. And since Shoshone Enterprises was a Native American owned company that would give us an advantage when it came to minority hiring requirements.

I hit the road running. A State of Wyoming Highway project in Lander was scheduled to bid next month. There was very little concrete work involved but I did notice a pretty good portion of highway fencing that was scheduled to be replaced. I had an opening! But in reviewing the specifications for the Highway Department's fencing, I noticed a click above the ordinary. Heavier gauge wire, wire stays, combination T-Bar and treated posts, and the number of wire strands was above what I had used in the past. I did a quick check with the local suppliers but was not able to locate the higher grade of materials specified.

I had accounts in Casper from my days as a contractor so I planned a day in Casper to pick their brains in hopes of locating the necessary materials. My very first stop was at Casper Concrete and BINGO my good buddy Vince knew right where to send me. He even called down and set up an appointment with the store manager. After a brief visit with Tom at Michael's Fence, I had the accounts set up and all the pricing I would need to submit my fencing bid.

When I began calling in my fencing numbers to the General Contractors on the bidders list, they were all dumbfounded with my numbers and the fact that we were a minority owned entity. I would find out later that my quotes were a little on the high side but most used my quote since we were local and Indian owned. The contract was awarded to Brasel & Sims another lander based contractor who had been around for years. I took the opportunity to meet Frank Sims which would prove very advantageous both on this project and in the foreseeable future. Shoshone Enterprises was in the fencing game almost without effort.

The highway project was a good beginning effort for me. I learned the methods and mannerisms of the office staff. DeAnn was very adept at running the office end of things. She handled all of the payroll as well as the accounts receivables. But their estimating practices were more from the seat of their pants than anything I had seen before. Dick was pretty sharp around equipment and operators but building construction was totally greek to him. It was a good thing the fencing project didn't start until the end of the summer because it would give everybody a chance to learn the strengths and weaknesses of each other. Dick knew his estimating abilities were weak. So what did he do, he purchased a total construction estimating computer program from an outfit in Denver. I had never heard of them but in digging into it, I found out that they were one of the biggest in the industry. And part of the package that had been purchased was a week long training seminar for four employees. I was completely taken back when my name was placed on the list. I had worked with the R. S. Means method and their estimating books but had little to no experience with computer estimating software.

For the next week, I was sent to Denver along with three up and coming employees of the Shoshone Tribe to learn all we could about the program we would be using. Denver has always been on the cutting edge of new and innovative construction styles and companies. We checked into a hotel right across the street from the office center for BiddWorx. We were treated like royalty from the get go. That first evening before class began was a prime rib dinner to write home about. They serve prime rib until we burst and all the fixings to boot.

When my three companions wanted to hit he local night club, I passed and headed to bed. The classes didn't start until 9 A.M. so I had time on my hands. One of the items included in the estimating package was a laptop computer for each attendee to use and take home. So I spent some time trying to cram fifteen years of computer training into those early morning periods while everybody else was still sleeping. Needless to say, I was a long ways behind everybody there. I understood more about the actual construction industry than most but my computer skills were practically non- existent. The one thing that I did realize from the training, was that an accounting system was integrated into the estimating package which would help us track the prices and manpower closer. The first thing I did when I walked back into the office back in Ft. Washakie was to sign DeAnn up for that same training session we had just attended. (She should have gone with us at the beginning)

WASHAKIE DAM RE-CONSTRUCTION

That summer began somewhat slowly, which gave me time to learn as much as I could about the company and the way the Business Council expected things to be run. The monthly meetings with the Business Council were intimidating to say the least but once I knew what they understood and expected the easier they became. John Washakie was definitely the leader of the Council and his abilities were many and varied. He was on top of all that went on around the reservation. It was in one of those first couple of council meetings that he informed Dick Ferris about the access road needed into the Washakie Reservoir. Shoshone Enterprises needed to widen and re-route a portion of the five mile long access road into the dam and it had to be done by the next spring.

The access road was no small undertaking. The existing road was barely wide enough for one vehicle to negotiate all the switchbacks up and over the divide that separated the reservoir from the town of Ft. Washakie. The configuration of the road would require a portion to be re-routed to avoid an outcropping of shale rock that blocked a widening effort. A BIA Engineer who had spent most of his career on the Wind River Indian Reservation was assigned to stake out the new route. He was a trusted advisor to the tribe and could be counted on not to disturb any more of the natural topography than absolutely necessary.

The engineer put on his hiking boots and spent a week studying and staking out the new road into the reconstruction site. It was a good job for an engineer because that road had to be wide enough and flat enough to transport 150,000 cy of structural fill over the divide without any accidents or road failures. In the meantime, Dick went shopping for a D-10 Cat. He was like a kid in a candy store. But the tribe had only given him authority to lease the equipment for a year. But still a D-10 Cat for his crew to put to as many uses as possible! Dick was in Seventh Heaven!

I can still picture Dick's smile as that transport arrived at the shop. The entire company was out to admire and drool over the shiny new bulldozer, all the way from that monstrous dozer blade in front to the massive ripper tooth on the tail end. Dick climbed into the cab with the transport driver to direct him to the base of the old Washakie Dam Road where they unloaded it. After checking all of the fluid levels and topping off the fuel tank, Dick slid on to the operator's seat and fired her up. Again instant gratification was splashed across Dick's face. He had the privilege of pushing the first yard of overburden away from the tiny road in anticipation for specification base course to be hauled in.

Over the next three months, the crew of operators all got their chance to put that dozer through her paces. The road was taking shape and really becoming a work of beauty. The dozer was also used to prepare the tribal pit above town for exporting hundreds of yards of pit run gravels along the course of that road to fill in the gullies that needed compactable materials to in turn place the base course needed to support the hours of axle loads that would be consumed with importing the rock and sand needed to rebuild the leaking dam itself.

While all of that work was going on in Ft. Washakie, the fencing crew was finally given the green light to begin replacing the five section of fence along Highway 287. Michael's Fence delivered the first load of posts and barbed wire when called and the eight man crew went to work. It was a good thing the crew was local because they knew what was underneath the topsoil near Lander. Boulders are a way of life for anybody who disturbs the soils along the Wind River Mountains. A two-man post hole digger and plenty of eight foot long pry bars are a necessity. But one by one each treated wood post was set and each steel T-bar posts were driven along the line that had been staked by the licensed surveyors.

I mad numerous inspection trips into Lander to double check their progress and get their feed back for any future projects. The crews threatened me with dire consequences if I ever bid another fencing job but they didn't complain much when their tidy pay checks showed up every two weeks. The job was a good one for all involved.

It was near the completion of the fencing project and the Washakie Dam Road rework that a major crisis arose for Shoshone Enterprises. Dick Ferris, the manager, suffered a major heart attack. He survived but was not able to continue with his managerial duties over the crew or the equipment. DeAnn took over the office management while Kenny stepped in to direct the equipment scheduling and maintenance. The various crew chiefs were responsible for the work load of each of their men. It was tough but everyone rose to the situation. It was several weeks later that I first saw Dick out on a short walk near the tribal complex. He looked good considering what he had been through. But his days with Shoshone Enterprise were all but finished.

That winter was spent finishing up several projects around the area and getting the haul road into Washakie Dam ready for the main event. The general contractor opened up a small branch office in Ft. Washakie with a job trailer set up at the dam itself. And of course the government had to move its equipment and personnel on to the project. At times I could actually see more inspectors and testing technicians than I could see workers performing the reconstruction. But hey, that's the federal government at work.

During those preparatory months before the actual re-hab work was spent obtaining permits and suppliers lined up. When I heard that 150,000 cy of sand and gravel needed to be imported to the site, I asked from where? They planned on purchasing these fill materials from local suppliers. I again asked, why? The tribe had an abundance of river bottom available and gravel pits everywhere. Why not supply all the materials themselves? I was told that they didn't have to means to screen and produce the specifications needed. My response was, " Then sub-contract it out to a company who can!"

I was asked to prepare a proposal identifying the gravel source, the bid tabulations for the crushing and screening, and the reclamation upon completion. I went to work again with a backhoe and operator from Shoshone Enterprise. In my mind, the most cost effective way to produce the aggregates and get them delivered to the site was in locating a gravel source as close as possible to the dam itself. That shouldn't be that hard since they owned practically every piece of ground along the many rivers nearby.

I conversed with the tribal entities about existing gravel pits. I scoured over dozens of maps identifying private and tribal lands. I finally narrowed my search to a half dozen locations that had good potential and access to a water source. I spent the better part of the following week digging test holes. I wanted to find a location that had lots of fine aggregate (sand) and very little overburden to remove to help hold the crushing costs as low as possible. I finally located the ideal spot right along the haul road less than three miles from the construction site.

With that piece of ground identified, I solicited crushing bids from a dozen firms that I had worked with over the years in hopes that three responsible quotations would be received. I was quite pleased when all the quotes came in at less than half the cost of importing these same materials from public gravel pits. A local company was awarded the contract and a new gravel pit was opened up by Rocky Mountain Crushing. When I had approached the Business Council with my proposal I had promised a royalty was to be paid to the landowner fro every yard of gravel removed from the new pit. That meant that the potential from $300,000-$400,000 would be paid to each and every landowner involved. Little did I imagine that the deed for the land being used would actually impact over twenty four tribal members!

But I had submitted the proposal so it was up to me to locate and get approval from all twenty four tribal members before we could break ground. DeAnn at the office was one of those tribal members and she was a tremendous help in identifying who to contact and where they actually lived. Like most reservations the addressing system leaves much to be desired. Word of mouth and landmarks were oft times all that I had to go by. But after hours of driving and door knocking, I finally had all the signatures needed. I can still see that 'deer in the headlights' look in many of their faces as I explained what was happening and the dollar amount each could expect to receive. I am sure many of them were thinking, 'Here we go again with another white man promise that will never happen!'

With the crushing and screening operation underway, a staging area at the dam was needed where each of the dozen different products could be stockpiled. I estimated that a five acre piece of ground could hold the desired quantities. The general contractor identified what he needed and permission was obtained to grub and prepare the land necessary. A fueling station was also located within easy distance to the site complete with a 10,000 gallon fuel tank and portable weighing scales. The DEQ was very particular about fuel containment and leaching effects. They were satisfied when the whole fueling area was fabricated over a double layer of 50 mil reinforced plastic.

A couple of interesting incidents took place as this staging area was being put together. The contractor moved a couple of twenty yard scrapers onto the site to strip and stockpile the topsoil on the staging area to the side for future reclamation work. One Monday as the foreman was driving up the haul road towards the dam he encounters one of his scrapers heading back towards town. He wheels his Ford truck around to follow the scraper. It is weaving all over the place and traveling at a very unsafe speed. Corner after corner were taken with fence posts and wire being shredded.

On one of these corners the scraper gets high centered whereupon the foreman barrels out of his pickup and runs to shut of the fuel lines of the scraper. With no fuel the scraper was dead in the water, out piles two Native American teenage girls about fifteen years of age and they were as drunk as skunks. The tribal police were called and the two guilty vandals were hauled away. As I listened to the foreman tell the story, I was flabbergasted. These two girls had managed to hot wire the scraper since no key was found. A scraper is a very complex as well as scary piece of equipment to run down the highway. It was a miracle in and of itself that nobody was hurt at all.

The next major snafu at the dam involved those same scrapers. The staging area for stockpiles, fueling, equipment storage, and parking was being leveled and the topsoil again was being placed along the Eastern slope away from the dam. Some of the tribal elders and their 'Medicine Men' came to the business council with a disturbance in their dreams at night. They asked me to investigate before a field trip of sorts was taken by the concerned tribal members. I took a day to drive and inspect for any wrong doings along the haul road and at the construction site itself.

The leisurely drive up the Washakie Dam road did not reveal anything out of the ordinary. I did see a couple of bald eagles, a red tailed hawk, and a lone coyote which I admired from a distance. The activity at the staging area was just about what I expected to see. Two scrapers were removing the overburden and topsoil from a large ten or eleven acre alcove on the downhill side of the basin that the reservoir was nestled inside of. The small stream that flowed out of the reservoir was running clear and uninhibited down the same course it had for years. The scene was well organized and well planned out. I did notice some small fire rings that were scattered periodically around the perimeter of the site. I personally walked over to investigate the fire ring closest to where I was parked. It was a bout two feet in diameter with a few softball size flat stones embedded in the exposed dirt. I didn't think too much more about it.

The following day a couple of tribal transportation vans were loaded up with elders from the tribe and council members for a site seeing trip along the same route I had traveled just the day before. I received an urgent phone call from the contractor at the dam site just before noon requiring my immediate presence at the staging area. Upon arriving I see the whole entourage of Native Americans scattered along the perimeter of the staging area kicking around several of the exposed fire rings. The scrapers had been parked along side the large stockpile of topsoil and parked just like they did at the close of work each day. I walked over to John Washakie to determine what the issue was.

The council members that were present included a member assigned to monitor the 'spiritual' affairs of the tribe. I had known each year he was directly in charge of the annual 'Pow-Wow' gathering that brought hundreds of Eastern Shoshone Tribal Members to a sacred ceremony. As I approached I could see that he was quite agitated. As

I stood quietly listening to the conversation, I picked out that words 'desecration' and 'sacrilege'. The contractor was also present and was being bombarded from every side with accusations and dissatisfaction. Something had really happened that I was not previously aware of.

The ensemble of tribal representatives were claiming that a sacred Ancestral Gathering place had been desecrated by the construction activities. They wanted the entire operation to stop work and leave immediately. The BIA and Federal officials that were present were frantically trying to ease the tensions manifest.

A combined meeting was convened at the main construction office to discuss any and all options. I was not included in the actual meeting itself but the bottom line that came out of that meeting was felt immediately. The construction at the dam site was being shut down until the Archeology staff from the University of Wyoming could get a team of specialists on-site. I had never been involved with archeologists before but the stories were rampant about what they can do and the power they have to change the course of any prehistoric site.

The very next day a dozen full sized vans with the University logo plastered on the doors arrived with what appeared to be every modern day electronic device used to open up a full scale archeological dig. The entire staging area was sectioned off and the staff and students proceeded to analysis the fire rings one by one.

Over the course of the next four hours I was to learn about the twentieth century's mode of preserving artifacts. The artifacts would be identified, dated, and cataloged before they would be returned to their original location. The days of removing any and all traces to a museum were long gone. They estimated that the entire 'find' would be recorded and isolated from any further disturbance in the next three to four weeks. The other work at the dam itself could proceed as planned. Whew! The reclamation project was back on schedule again. If anything it would allow the crushing and screening operation to get ahead of the demand whereas they had been barely able to meet the basic daily demand for sand and specification gravels.

CONSTRUCTION HICCUPS

At the end of the month, the archeological team, from the university, was packing up their entire array of fact-finding gadgets and headed towards their next dig. They did leave a report of their findings however. The campfire rings were less than five hundred years old and were probably made by Native Americans that were making tools and weapons for their tribe out of Feldspar rock that was located not to distant from there. The remnants of spearheads, arrowheads, and scraping tools that were found did not change any already documented evidence about the inhabitants of the Wind Rivers. No human remains were found with only small mammal skeletal items remaining behind. WOW!

But even with the extra crushing time, the quantities needed were becoming an urgent problem. So once again I was sent on a hunting exploration throughout the Indian Reservation. Reject sand or better yet washed sand was needed immediately. I did locate several Indian-owner sources of reject sand. I secured samples from each source and had the testing people run screen tests on each. The best possibility was located on the outskirts of Riverton. The thousand yards of sand was a finer gradation than what was being used but would work! But the haul was over fifty miles one-way. The contractor needed the product as soon as possible so permits and signatures were obtained. Every hauler on the reservation along with some local licensed rigs was hired. The thousand-yard stockpile was hauled to the Washakie Dam and none to soon.

As the reconstruction of the Washakie Dam was winding down, I was placed in charge of the reclamation effort. I made contact with the local BLM officials to identify the best dry land seed variety of grasses they felt would re-vegetate the roadsides and staging areas the fastest and longest. I solicited bids for hydro-seeding the hundreds of acres that needed to be covered. It was quite interesting between the different methods and recommendations offered. But a local part-time hydro-seeder, secured the bid and ordered the mixture of mulch and seed in compliance with the BLM specifications. It was quite amazing to watch the unit working. In one moment it was bare ground, and the following instance it was totally green. (The mulch and the bonding agent had a green dye included) whaa-la the whole mountainside was instant beautiful.

Now all I had to do was redistribute the royalty checks to all of the Shoshone Tribal members that owned a percentage in the lands and gravels mined at the new pit. There I was with over five hundred thousand dollars in checks retracing my steps to each and every person that had signed the agreement. I can still remember several of their faces as I handed them their portion and had them acknowledge it with another signature. The facial expressions varied from total disbelief, others of pleasant surprise, and finally those who couldn't wait to head to Vegas. Those who had forbearance and restraint would have a tidy nest egg for the future while others might be able to remember the great time they had blowing it at the casinos in Vegas (depending on how snockered they were at the time). I felt like I had truly helped many, many residents of the Wind River Indian Agency better their situation just a little.

ESTIMATOR FULL TIME FOR THE SHOSHONE TRIBE

The next few months would be spent bidding and looking for more tribal work. I didn't have to wait long. The Tribal Business Council saw the large influx of royalty monies from the sand and gravel reserves right under their feet. They found out I had crusher experience and they already had an active gravel pit just north of town. I was sent out to try and locate a rock crusher to assist the business possibilities.

I didn't have to look far as Brasel & Sims a road contractor based out of Lander had a portable cone crusher they wanted to sell. It had a lot of features that I felt were advantageous to the Shoshone Tribal Council. It was portable which allowed it to be transported to many gravel sites on the reservation. They were including a feeder hopper and multiple screening conveyors, which would allow for greater flexibility. And it had a triple vibratory screen included, which had piping for the use of washing the final products. It looked like a

CONSTRUCTION HICCUPS

sound business investment to me. I made my recommendation to the Business Council and then stood back to see what happened.

The owners met for the better part of an afternoon trying to work out an agreement with the Shoshone Tribe. When they emerged from their chambers, they were all smiles. The deal had been finalized. A bonus was included in the negotiations. A training period would be offered to help bring the Native American crew up to speed on the smooth operation of the crusher. And to save a few bucks the Shoshone Enterprises truck fleet would transport the cone and all the conveyors themselves. This was going to be a decision both hazardous, detrimental, and beneficial to the success of the venture.

The cone crusher and conveyors were located a few short miles South of Lander. A transport of thirty miles was nothing at all to the operators from Shoshone Enterprises. But wait until you hear what transpired!

The cone crusher was mobilized first. It was hitched to the newest Mack rig the tribe owned. Gerald the most experienced operator of the bunch pulled the load up to the crest of the hill, where he parked the rig and proceeded back to help secure the remaining four semi-loads of hoppers and conveyors. As the fifteen man crew as engaged in securing each and every axle load, a thunderous roar was heard off to our left. We all turned towards the sound and noticed immediately that the truck and portable crusher had disappeared! At the same point of the loud roar, a huge column of dust arose out of that gully. The trucks brakes had failed and the entire load, crusher and all, were lying at the bottom of the thirty-foot ravine! I can still see the looks of total disbelief on the faces of the entire crew. A simple task turned sour by nobody's fault. Accidents happen! Thank heaven nobody was hurt by the runaway transport.

Brasel & Sims offered to mobilize their 30-ton crane to help extract the wreckage out of the gully. And for the better part of that week, piece after piece of equipment was hoisted out of the ravine and transported to the tribe's gravel pit above Ft. Washakie. I was pretty sure the insurance coverage of the Business Council would cover the loss but I was more concerned about the condition of the crusher itself. It was decided to hire the manufacturer of the cone crusher to analyze the damage and rebuild the unit from the ground up.

Jimmy T. was sent out to head up the rework. He was an older gentleman with a slight paunch on him and slightly balding but he knew his stuff. After a week's demolition of the crusher, he asked for a conference before he started the reassembly. He sat us all down and very bluntly informed us that the crusher had not been maintained properly before the accident. Point by point he showed us the abused portions of the cone. Once he had completed his diagnosis, he sat down waiting on a decision from the Business Council on how much they were willing to spend on the repairs. I never did find out what the final bill was or who ended up paying what, but the decision was to rebuild it for the long haul. "It will be just like having a new cone crusher when we're finished," was the last thing I heard.

It took Jimmy T. and his crew the better part of six weeks to get the new parts and re-assemble the cone crusher. I stopped in ever so often to check on their progress and was pleased every time I did. These guys knew what they were doing. The last thing that Jimmy T. did before he left was to pull me aside and explain to me that the feeder hopper for the crusher would be the 'bottle-neck' of the whole operation. And I needed to upgrade that piece of equipment if I ever wanted this crusher to make the 200 ton/hour it is capable of producing. And with that little bit of advice they headed down the road.

The plant and the Native American operators were off and running full steam ahead. The Business Council had set their goal of 100,000 tons of crushed specification road gravel by next spring. (They wanted to rebuild the Ethete-Ft. Washakie roadway) A lofty goal but very obtainable with the source and pit conditions at their disposal. All they had to do was keep that crusher running 50% of the time. So Ben and his operators were eager and willing. But here were two things standing in their way.

The first was success and the second was Mother Nature. The crushing crew really got off to a great start. The crusher was everything they had promised. The three front-end loaders had a tough time keeping up. But an early spring up-slope weather pattern socked into the basin. In a 72-hour period of time, Ft Washakie received over sixty inches of snow. Every piece of equipment that Shoshone Enterprises could lay its hands on was used in digging tribal members out from that monster storm. And that included the loaders at the pit too.

To add insult to injury, just as soon as the roads were passable again, the wind changed directions and for the next two days it blew all those same roads shut again. The equipment and manpower was stretched to the limit. The weather did settle down again, but only to find another problem at the crusher/pit. While the operators were off clearing roadways, the plant should have been receiving much needed maintenance.

Come to find out, the good money these men were receiving, affected their judgment. Instead of taking care of their families or saving for tough times ahead, the money was used to purchase marijuana and other banned substances. Shoshone Enterprises had a 0% drug policy in place. These men were dismissed and replacements needed to be located. That crushing goal of 100,000 tons was really starting to look like 'pie in the sky'. But new employees were located and a training program was implemented for six new members of the Eastern Shoshone Tribe.

During this series of events that involved the crusher, I was busy trying to locate additional work for the other employees of Shoshone Enterprises. I had been watching the market as well as the Dodge Reports for any high-end government contracts that were in the immediate future. Two such bid solicitations hit the streets about the same time. The Indian Housing Authority wanted to build a dozen scattered low-income homes at various locations on the Wind River Indian Reservation. This particular project was set aside for Indian-owned small business entities. Shoshone Enterprises fit the parameters to the 'T'. But these contracts always received a huge amount of publicity and would require a 'bare bones' bid to land it. We were the only resident contractor qualified to submit a bid, which would give us a slight edge. The prevailing Davis-Bacon wage rates would also be attached to the contract. The contractors would all be working with the same set of standards!

A second advertised bid was being circulated around the area. The Arapaho Business Council had hired an architect to design a new tribal office complex in Ethete. This was a lot closer than Arapaho but it did pose a small conflict. Special permission was needed for Shoshone Enterprises to bid the project. The Shoshone and the Arapaho tribes both resided on the same reservation but an unwritten code existed between the two tribes. The Shoshones controlled the Western side of the reservation and the Arapahos controlled the Eastern side. Ethete was right on the imaginary boundary between the two nations.

I met with the chairman of the Arapaho Business Council to see if a compromise could be reached. He was totally against any such agreement until he discovered that Shoshone Enterprises had several Arapaho members working for them. And when I told him of my satisfaction with the work ethic of Ronnie Oldman (his nephew) he was sold on the package. I knew a ready supply of Arapaho workers would be at Ronnie's call. So again I had an edge when it came to both upcoming bids. I would have to better organize the office staff since the two bids opened within two weeks of each other.

I developed a list of suppliers and sub-contractors that I knew would turn in their best numbers. I then put DeAnn to notifying each one on that list to make sure they had our contact information and the time of the bid opening. I then located cardboard boxes large enough to contain two or three dozen bid quotation forms. On each of these boxes, I wrote the name of the bid section along with the section number. I had a dozen different categories so I located a dozen different boxes. As the bids would come in, each one would be placed in the appropriate box. This way all I had to do was sort the bids from lowest to highest to arrive at the best number submitted. It had worked for me in the past and I showed the system to the gals at Shoshone Enterprises.

As the estimator for the Shoshone Tribe I had to study each section in order to formulate a reasonable idea whether a bid was 'responsible' or not. There is more to a bid than just the low number! Their ability to perform, their financial soundness, how many Indian employees they employ, and any conflict of interest I knew about are items I had to prepare for. I also had to identify which areas of work Shoshone Enterprises could perform and then formulate that bid by and in of itself. I had a short two week window to accomplish this task. (Remember that I have two separate bids within two weeks of each other)

SCATTERED HUD HOMES

The day of the first bid (Scattered Home Sites) found me at the office before the sun broke the horizon. I did not want any surprises. To my advantage were the few bids I had already received. I had a solid bid for the Electrical Work as well as the Heating and Cooling Work. Any more bids would help narrow down the decision. I had my own Shoshone Enterprises numbers in front of me too. I did get a chuckle when a few numbers were called in on sections that Shoshone Enterprises always performed in house. I guess they didn't do their homework. The bids had to be submitted by 2 P.M., which gave me a little breathing room. The office staff all showed up on time and were prepared to receive their marching orders. Here we go, ready or not!

I had directed the office help to stop receiving bids at 1 P.M. in order to give up that last hour to organize each section and formulate our final number. The phones didn't start ringing until 11 A.M. and then it was a two- hour ordeal in answering phones and fax lines. Each verbal quote had to be written down and any exceptions recorded. Those along with the faxed quotations were pigeon-holed in their respective cardboard category box. Around noon I asked DeAnn if we had bids for every section? She turned around white as a sheet when she noticed an empty box for Sheetrock and Taping. I quickly consulted my master sub list to see who had promised bids. A couple of quick phone calls to the business was all that was needed. As the one o'clock hour approached we realized that we had numbers for every building section. A sense of total relief flooded over me. Now I had an hour to analyze each bid and decide what our bottom line bid was going to be.

The process wasn't that complicated due to the experience I had with many of the contractors who were submitting quotes. It was easy to set aside the high bids and those quotes I knew could not handle the work. But as the hour ticked away I was seeing a potential conflict brewing. The quotations from several subs had glaring deficiencies in major areas. I did not have the time to review each bid over the phone. So I used a trick I had seen other contractors use in the past. I added another ten percent to their quote and then I entered the name of Shoshone Enterprises as the trade name of the apparent low bidder. This would allow me to negotiate the final number with the parties involved at a future date.

This could prove to be dangerous if a solid number could not be agreed upon forcing Shoshone Enterprises to perform the work specified. But I was willing to take the chance. At five minutes before the hour, I phoned my man at the housing office and relayed my final tabulation. He wrote it down on the proper line after repeating it to me twice. I wanted there to be no mistakes. My man then stayed as each of the bids were opened and read out loud. He wrote down each and every bid number. There were six bids submitted and we were the apparent low bidder! Three cheers for Shoshone Enterprises!

The following day I declined to talk to all the bidders wanting to know how they had done. I just didn't know until I had time to review each and every quote submitted personally for the second time. I also had to convince myself that I wanted the bid. I truly wanted the job but if I had a glaring mistake in addition or subtraction it could really hurt the company. I was over joyed to see only a 2 % difference from my bid and the next three bidders. It had been really close! By the end of that day I had personally notified each and every bidder of their standing on the upcoming project. It was heart warming to hear most accept their rejection as gentlemen but there were always a few who swore they would take it to a higher level and get even. Sad…so Sad!!!

CONSTRUCTION HICCUPS

I received our notice of award the very next week. I still had a ton of forms to complete and mail. (This is a government project you know.) As I notified each and every contractor with whom I planned on doing business with, I kept coming up short on one line. I was not having any success in landing a sheetrock company that could satisfy all my demands. The timing always seemed to be the key stumbling block. We always agreed on the dollars needed but they would not commit to the time schedule I attached to the contracts. I negotiated the items with every firm that bid the hanging and taping of the homes. No takers! I was between a rock and a hard place. I was resolved to make this contract a win-win for the Tribe and Shoshone Enterprises. I opted to complete the items 'in-house'. I had my work cut out for me.

The first place I looked was at local people that were skilled in the trade but no longer able or willing to perform the labor-intensive task identified. I was in luck and located a retired taper that would work with me on the training. The first thing he wanted was a willing crew and all their own tools. I had him write down the bare bones tools needed to complete the job. I was completely blown away when he handed me a fifty-item list of the very basic tools he required. But I had made my bed and now I had to sleep in it. What made matters even worse was the two jobs we were working on both needed the same tools and materials at the very same time! I would need two of everything!

So arrangements were made and I ordered taping blades, hawks, boxes, banjos, bazookas, and stilts for the two crews that we would train. I did have a couple of workers that had some experience and they quickly became my lead men on the projects. Our first house was ready to have the sheetrock hung and the taping to follow. Eddie, my trainer, was eager and willing to train his new recruits. So with eight men in attendance, we began the training sessions. To say that things were moving slow would be an understatement. The men were willing but what experience they had was of the wrong kind. A complete re-training was in order. But after the second week, the crew chiefs were getting the hang of it. (Excuse the pun)

The hanging crew was off and running. Now the taping crew would get their chance. I was quite pleased at the guys I had selected. They were meticulous enough to really do a first rate job. Eddie spent the necessary time with them and the entire training program was the talk of the reservation. I had dozens of Native Americans interested in learning this trade. It was a good thing because one by one each of the original trainees became interested in some other pursuit except for my lead man. I was completely satisfied with Rocky's work ethics and his abilities. I had a keeper!

ARAPAHO TRIBAL COMPLEX IN ETHETE

The Arapaho Business Chambers bid went quite a bit differently than the Scattered Sites bid had just two weeks previous. News travels fast and the word was Shoshone Enterprises will do anything to land this project. I am not sure I would do anything to secure the bid but I was committed to both the Shoshone and Arapaho people to give it my best shot. It was more of a traditional project. One building with the associated site work in one location. When we went through the same bidding sequence as with the Scatter Sites bid, we were able to utilize a completely different set of sub- contractors. This would prove to be a great advantage in the long run.

On bid day, we found out that we were only bidding against one other bidder and they were non-Indian. I don't know if the Business Council would have awarded the project to them or not. I didn't have to find out because Shoshone Enterprises was the low bidder of record. But a big discrepancy existed between my numbers and that of the second bidder. The architect of record asked that the project be re-bid! After a lengthy discussion on the issue, I convinced the Architect and the Business Council to compare my figures with the Architect's estimate and explain the wide range in costs. In so doing, it was discovered that my numbers were less than 1 % off the estimate. The Architect had his reasons but I still do not understand them to this day. The Business Council went ahead and awarded this contract to Shoshone Enterprises.

The first thing that I did after we received the contract was to appoint Ronnie Oldman the project superintendent. He was the right man for the job. The employees responded well to his leadership and experience. The office complex was underway. It was a good thing that Ronnie was in charge because a huge portion of my time was spent on the Scattered Housing project.

The ten houses included in the project were scattered across a hundred square miles of reservation land. There was a hose near Crowheart and then the next was on the opposite side of Riverton. I was really churning up the miles as I visited each home on a weekly basis. It seemed like the harder I tried to maintain control, the behinder I got. I decided to try out one of the office staff as an assistant supervisor. Brett was a eager helper in the past but did he have the organizational abilities needed. There was only one way to find out.

I placed him over the three homes located within twenty miles of Ft. Washakie. Then I took a step back to watch what would happen. The sub- contractors and crews working responded well to his supervision and direction. My telephone log decreased over half as the bulk of the issues on these homes were handled by Brett. All I had to do was review with Brett once or twice a week the material demands and scheduling issues that would surface. Brett was going to make a great replacement when the time was right.

I had two assistant superintendents in Ronnie and Brett. Each one had his strengths and weaknesses but I felt they could overcome these with proper guidance and mentoring. I still had some work to do with the office personnel. DeAnn was a great office manager but she needed to learn more about bidding and organizing a pool of suppliers and contractors she could draw on for help and problem solving.

The next bid that Shoshone Enterprises was eligible to perform was on the Ethete Highway Reconstruction. The scope of that project consisted in re-paving close to thirty miles of existing highway between Ethete and Ft. Washakie. It also included several concrete bridges and close to ten miles of new fencing. The concrete work and fencing was right down Shoshone Enterprises' alley. So I rolled up my sleeves once again to help DeAnn put this bid in order.

We pulled out the R.S. Means bid catalog and reviewed every step needed in identifying labor totals and quantities. We identified what formwork would be needed and reviewed our quantity takeoffs several times to make sure we were not forgetting anything. Supplier prices were obtained from Casper, Riverton, and Lander. We organized each and every requirement and phoned in our quotation to each of the dozen contractors. I recognized most of them from past projects but there were a couple of firms I had never heard of.

As the opening was in its final stages, I received a strange phone call from a friend in Casper. He cautioned me about giving my numbers to Clawson Construction. He claimed that they had bid with them before and that firm had 'shopped ' their numbers to a sister company that ended up getting the contract. I had heard of companies doing this around the state but had never been involved to any degree. A general contractor wants to use their sister company and waits until the apparent low prices come across their desks. Then a quick phone call to the sister company with the number and all of a sudden the sister company becomes the lowest bidder by the slimmest of margins.

Well, this happened at Ethete, when Clawson Construction came in as the apparent low bidder. I checked with the estimators from a couple of other firms and they acknowledged that Shoshone Enterprises had the best numbers for the work quoted. But Clawson Construction ended up getting the job with their sister company doing the same work that Shoshone Enterprises should have been performing.

I sat down with DeAnn and reviewed the bids along with our estimates. We had the right procedures, the perfect numbers, but did not get the contract. She was very disappointed as was I but all we could do was move on to the next project to see if it would turn out better for us.

I would not ever see that happen. John Washakie was released as the head of the Shoshone Business Council and his successor saw my salary as a way to help the tribe to save on money expenditures. My contract was not renewed and I was sent packing. My time with the Native American tribes on the Wind River Indian Reservation had come to a close.

EPILOGUE

Now that my children had all graduated from high school, we decided to travel while we worked. I had been a Commercial Superintendent right out of college. We had an offer to return to that position with an Idaho based contractor. At first, the jobs were in Wyoming, but then a company hired us to work the Western United States. Our children would be flown to see us every three months or we could fly to see them. The money was good and we would get to see some of the country around us. So we bought a fifth wheel trailer, sold our land and home and ventured on the road to see Commercial Construction as it really existed west of the Mississippi River.

www.ingramcontent.com/pod-product-compliance
Ingram Content Group UK Ltd.
Pitfield, Milton Keynes, MK11 3LW, UK
UKHW022226230426
12048UKWH00016BA/1091